So You Want to Be a

Commercial Airline Pilot

Here's the Info You Need

D0807863

By Captain Jack Watson
Revised by Danielle Thorne

SO YOU WANT TO BE A COMMERCIAL AIRLINE PILOT: HERE'S THE INFO YOU NEED

1405 SW 6th Avenue • Ocala, Florida 34471 • Phone 800-814-1132 • Fax 352-622-1875
Website: www.atlantic-pub.com • Email: sales@atlantic-pub.com
SAN Number: 268-1250

Library of Congress Cataloging-in-Publication Data

Names: Thorne, Danielle, author.
Title: So you want to be a commercial airline pilot—here's the info you need / by Danielle Thorne.
Description: Ocala, Florida : Atlantic Publishing Group, Inc, [2017] | Includes bibliographical references and index.
Identifiers: LCCN 2017057161 (print) | LCCN 2017057963 (ebook) | ISBN 9781620232101 (ebook) | ISBN 9781620232095 (pbk. : alk. paper) | ISBN 9781620232521 (library edition : alk. paper) | ISBN 162023209X (alk. paper)
Subjects: LCSH: Airplanes—Piloting—Vocational guidance. | Aeronautics, Commercial—Vocational guidance.
Classification: LCC TL561 (ebook) | LCC TL561 .T496 2017 (print) | DDC 629.13023—dc23
LC record available at https://lccn.loc.gov/2017057161

Printed in the United States

PROJECT MANAGER: Danielle Lieneman • dlieneman@atlantic-pub.com
INTERIOR LAYOUT: Nicole Sturk • nicolejonessturk@gmail.com

Reduce. Reuse.
RECYCLE.

A decade ago, Atlantic Publishing signed the Green Press Initiative. These guidelines promote environmentally friendly practices, such as using recycled stock and vegetable-based inks, avoiding waste, choosing energy-efficient resources, and promoting a no-pulping policy. We now use 100-percent recycled stock on all our books. The results: in one year, switching to post-consumer recycled stock saved 24 mature trees, 5,000 gallons of water, the equivalent of the total energy used for one home in a year, and the equivalent of the greenhouse gases from one car driven for a year.

Over the years, we have adopted a number of dogs from rescues and shelters. First there was Bear and after he passed, Ginger and Scout. Now, we have Kira, another rescue. They have brought immense joy and love not just into our lives, but into the lives of all who met them.

We want you to know a portion of the profits of this book will be donated in Bear, Ginger and Scout's memory to local animal shelters, parks, conservation organizations, and other individuals and nonprofit organizations in need of assistance.

– Douglas & Sherri Brown,
President & Vice-President of Atlantic Publishing

Table of Contents

Introduction

The alarm blares. A bedside clock reads 4:30. Although it still feels like the middle of the night, a shadow slips out of bed and stumbles into the bathroom for a quick shower. Within minutes, the early riser takes a clean and neatly pressed uniform off its hanger and puts it on. The bags are already packed. A drive to the airport will only take 20 minutes.

There's no time for a hot breakfast. On the way to the airport, a few phone calls make sure everything is on schedule. The car is parked in an employee parking lot, and an airport shuttle bus drives the rest of the way to the airport. It stops at a special entrance for employees. After going through security and presenting the right identification, the early riser takes an escalator to an underground train that will stop at different stations inside the airport, called terminals. At the right stop, there is a short walk down a long hallway past restaurants and restrooms to the right gate. Customers are waiting in the gate area where they can see an airplane parked outside the tall, glass windows.

The ticket agents wave hello from their desk. The employee passes through a secure door and walks a few more strides down a jetway connecting the airport's gate to the airplane parked outside. Passing through the open door to the aircraft a brief hello is exchanged with a flight crewmember who has already arrived. Inside the cockpit, the left chair is empty and waiting.

This employee is a commercial airline pilot, and he or she will see the sun rise above the clouds this morning in their first few hours at work. By the time they return home the next day, they will have flown hundreds of passengers from one part of the world to another in a matter of hours — voyages that once took months or even years.

Do you love to fly? Do you have a need for speed? If so, you may be perfect for a career in **aviation**. In 1986, being a pilot became as cool as ever when Paramount Pictures released the hit movie, *Top Gun*, about a military pilot training at the elite "Top Gun Naval Fighter Weapons School." Today, major airlines in the United States employ thousands of pilots who fly aircraft all over the world, day and night. Like *Top Gun* pilots, they are the best of the best.

Considering salary, benefits, and experiences, it's more than a cool job, it's an exciting career. Anyone with the dream, desire, and as some pilots call it, "the right stuff", can make it as a commercial airline pilot. Having the right stuff to become a pilot includes a love of flight, commitment, education, training, and lots and lots of testing. And that's just the beginning.

This book is a guide for what it takes to become a commercial airline pilot. It includes things you should know, what you will need to prepare to learn, sample questions from testing, and other educational material. It also offers stories and advice from real life professionals from the cockpit and in the aviation industry.

CHAPTER 1

The Right Stuff

A pilot is responsible for all of the operations and passengers aboard an aircraft. Unlike most other jobs, things happen so fast there is no time for research or discussion. There are often only seconds to make a decision that could be the difference between life and death. This means no opportunity for help or advice from their radios or their crew. Pilots, especially the captain of a commercial airliner, are said to be made, not born.

From the cockpit

"When I was very young, about five or six, my dad got his private pilots' license. He would take me flying with him and put me on his lap and let me 'fly' the plane. My first year in college I needed one more credit, so I found an aviation class that I thought would be easy enough to fill my schedule. The first week of class, the instructor invited us to come to the airport for a ride in an airplane. I think I was hooked after that flight." ■

Some pilots say learning to fly can feel like being thrown into the deep end of a pool to learn to swim. It may be dangerous and even cost lives on rare occasions. Pilots must be able to stay cool under pressure, stay calm in scary situations, and have excellent communication skills. They should be able to get along with all types of personalities. An airline captain sets the mood for a professional, happy, and efficient flight crew that can make a flight great or miserable.

 **Fast Fact**

The Federal Aviation Administration of the United States (FAA) is the branch of the federal government that makes the laws, rules, and guidelines that control aviation.

Becoming a pilot is an investment. It will take years of study, training, work, and a great deal of money just to become a **Commercial Pilot**. Finally, after acquiring well over a thousand hours flight time you will earn the all-important **Airline Transportation Pilot Rating** (ATP). This rating allows you to fly as captain of a commercial airliner. To acquire the ATP you must pass a long and difficult test given by the **Federal Aviation Administration** (FAA). Passing this test will send you on your way to one day becoming a commercial airline pilot.

The Captain's Chair

Becoming a pilot means someday you may wear the respected four stripes on your shirt sleeves that shows you are a pilot-in-command, or Captain. You will be responsible for the lives of your passengers, crew, and the aircraft you fly.

 ***Fast Fact***

The captain sits in the left seat of the cockpit.

The captain position is the result of years of training, testing, and waiting. Commercial airlines promote their pilots to captains based on seniority.

In each company, the captain with the highest seniority, meaning the pilot who has worked for the company the longest, usually flies the largest aircraft. He has the first choice of equipment and the first choice of which routes to fly. The most senior captain is also the highest paid. This is because the number one-ranked pilot in a company is expected to be one of the most experienced **aviators** in the pilot ranks.

Fast Fact

Pilots hoping to become captains must wait years and years, because most airline companies have seniority lists that are thousands of employees long!

Seniority isn't always about who flies the best. Pilots usually work with a special organization called a union. It protects them and their jobs by bargaining with management. Unions help make the contracts, or agreements, with the companies pilots work for. The agreement sets the rules for the job and also how much the pilot will be paid.

From the cockpit

"The best trip I ever had was my first flight as Captain." ∎

Pilots with lower seniority usually fly smaller planes. They may also have the hardest work schedules and trips. This means less pay, but it is a part of the process of learning to fly different aircraft in different situations. It also provides valuable experience.

If that doesn't sound safe, don't worry. Aviation experts say you are safe flying with all commercial airline pilots. Pilots and captains must meet a set of professional requirements. They are also tested regularly to make sure they have "the right stuff" to continue doing their job.

Do you have the "right stuff?" Below are a few questions similar to what you may find on the required Airline Transportation Rating test given by the FAA.

- What is the purpose of ground spoilers?

- Which engine is the 'critical' engine of a twin-engine airplane?

- What is the stall speed of an airplane?

- What is the effect on total drag of an aircraft if the airspeed decreases?

- What is the maximum speed during takeoff that the pilot may abort the takeoff?

Life Changes

The moment you become a commercial airline pilot, your life and the lives of your family will go through many changes not everyone will understand. First, you will see your partner, children, parents, and the rest of your family much less than workers in other career fields. This means you will likely miss important events like birthdays, anniversaries, christenings, funerals, parties, holidays, and some family vacations. It will be difficult to be there for children when they have school plays, sports, and dance recitals.

Fast Fact

When a pilot is first hired by an airline, he or she will go through a test or trial period called "probation."

Pilots are not paid very much when they first start out. In the first year it might be necessary to work a second job to keep food on the table. Starting pay is getting better, but for many it's still less than $25,000 per year.

Today, after taxes, medical insurance, and other expenses are subtracted from their paychecks, some new hire airline pilots are left with less than $1,200 dollars a month of spendable income. This is a tough salary to live on if you have a family. Afterward, during the next year, pay goes up considerably.

From the cockpit

"I worked with a company that provided maintenance parts for fighter aircraft. My wife was from a military pilot family, and she suggested that I apply to the Air Force. I did, and the rest is history." ∎

Flying new equipment can often mean a change of home base. This can result in a family move, or if flying solo, a need to find a place closer to work. During their career path, a pilot can live in places like Seattle, San Diego, Las Vegas, Houston, Detroit, or Daytona Beach at different times.

Virtually any city with commercial airline service can become home. Commercial airline pilots can typically fly for free on other airlines using "jump seat privileges." This lets them use a seat in the cockpit for free to get to and from a destination. Most of the time, moving is voluntary and will be paid for by the airline. This kind of moving around is necessary to step up to bigger airplanes and bigger paychecks.

Another life change that comes with your aviation career will be a new diet. Pilots learn to love airline food and also the fast food served at airports. Most people gain weight because there isn't a lot of time to plan meals or find healthy options when on the run from one city to another.

There will be extra expenses, too. The first few paychecks of a new pilot must pay for uniforms. This includes hats, ties, and shirts, and can cost hundreds and hundreds of dollars. They will have to be cleaned professionally at a dry cleaner, and that costs money, too.

From the cockpit

"I always liked planes. I grew up building model airplanes and keeping my eyes fixed on the sky. I knew the stats of airplanes like most kids knew the stats of baseball or football. For my 14th birthday, my stepbrother arranged for his dad to take me flying. After we returned to the airport, I told them I wanted to be a pilot." ■

Why do they do it? Pilots fly because they love it. Flight, even in a commercial airliner, means high speed and heavenly scenery like sunrises, sunsets, and thunderstorms. Becoming an airline captain can be the proudest moment of a plane lover's career.

CHAPTER 2

Planes and People to Fly Them

Pilots should not only understand how to operate an airplane, they should have a good understanding of the history of aviation and how airplanes have changed from the first inventions to the aircraft we have today.

Science credits modern flight as originating in 1783 with hot air balloons. **Joseph-Michael and Jacques-Ètienne Montgolfier** began the first hot air balloon flights that lifted pilots up off of the earth. The first tests kept the balloon tethered to the ground, but within a year the ropes were cut, and Man traveled through the sky.

 ***Fast Fact***

The first powered flight is believed to have been achieved by a steam-powered airship on September 24th, 1852. The pilot, Henri Giffard, traveled about 16 miles from Paris to Trappes at around six miles per hour.

Most people credit Orville and Wilbur Wright of North Carolina for the first flight in 1903. The Wright brothers built a plane called the *Wright Flyer*. It flew 12 seconds and 120 feet. It opened the door to aviation in the United States. The brothers' accomplishment is sometimes called "the first powered flight," but experts argue about whether or not to give them credit. Critics feel it's important to be more specific, re-naming it "the first manned, powered, heavier-than-air and (to some degree) controlled" success.

Airplanes improved between 1905 and 1918 thanks to inventors, engineers, and World War I. The U.S. Post Office (USPS) was the first to think of using flight for commercial, or business, purposes. USPS began sending mail by air to speed up the delivery of letters and packages. This increased the interest in airplane design and production. It also meant more pilots were needed, which provided training and jobs.

The plan to transport mail by air had a rough start at first because the converted planes did not do well in bad weather. Eventually, some of the early mail planes were used to train pilots in World War I. After the war ended, larger planes were available, and they flew faster and safer.

 ***Fast Fact***

By 1924, a letter mailed in New York could arrive in California in about two days. This not only made it easier for family and friends to communicate, it made it easier for businesses to exchange money and mail important documents.

Using airplanes to deliver mail became so popular the skies became busy, but there were few rules or laws. In 1925, the **Contract Air Mail Act** organized the country's mail service under a group of private companies called **contractors**. Soon after, a government organization was formed to make laws about building and operating airplanes. It was called the Air Commerce Act, and it also made rules for pilots. These new rules helped improve aircraft design and safety. It also caused a rapid growth and development in aviation that improved technology. Airplanes became faster and lighter and flew better than ever.

The First Pilots

Early pioneers in aviation weren't just intelligent and determined – they were brave, too. Learning to fly a machine took study, training, and a great deal of experience in the air. Flying could be exciting, even triumphant, but it could also be deadly.

There are many pilots who accomplished great firsts in the name of discovery and progress. Most notable is the famous war hero, James Doolittle. On September 24, 1929, Lieutenant James Doolittle made the first instrument takeoff, flight, and landing at Mitchel Field in Garden City, New York. His responses to a combination of electronic signals and airplane instruments permitted the first successful "blind flight."

 **Fast Fact**

Blind flight means flying only with instruments to guide you. It is a necessary skill for when there is bad or foggy weather out the windows.

This experiment by Lieutenant Doolittle represented a huge leap forward for all of aviation. It meant piloting an airplane without looking at the ground would be possible using only the instruments in the cockpit for attitude reference and navigation. As for Doolittle, he would later lead a famous raid over Tokyo, Japan, during World War II. He received the **Medal of Honor** and retired a Four-Star General in the United States Air Force.

Another man of that era, Charles A. Lindbergh, would also become an aviation legend. He is famous for flying the first nonstop solo flight from New York to Paris in 1927. Lindbergh began as a **wingwalker**, parachutist, and eventual mail pilot, for the Robertson Air Corporation. After his successful transatlantic flight to Paris, he continued to pilot, making a successful and much-needed survey flight in 1931 from New York to China with several stops along the way.

 **Fast Fact**

Walking out across an airplane's wing while it is in the air became a stunt called wingwalking in the 1920s. It was performed at many air shows then and is still a dangerous stunt dared today.

Aviation also spread across the American continent thanks to men like Noel Wien of Minnesota. He is given credit for introducing flight to Alaska in the 1920s. He flew to Anchorage when he was only 25-years-old, in a plane with a cockpit open to the air. That's a cold flight because the average temperature of Alaska in April of 1920 recorded at 29 degrees![1] He was the first man in Alaska to fly up north of the Arctic Circle. With only a few maps and no radio, Wien made travel a possibility in a harsh state the size of a small country.

The most famous female pilot, who proved to the world women could fly, too, was Amelia Earhart. She was born in 1897 in Kansas, not too long before the Wright brothers flew their airplane in North Carolina. Earhart may have been the 16th woman to earn a pilot's license, but she was the first

---

1. Intellicast, n.d.

woman to fly across the Atlantic Ocean. She next became the first person to fly over both the Atlantic and Pacific, but she did not complete a mission to circle the entire globe. Earhart is believed to have died somewhere in the Pacific islands around the equator, possibly in 1937 after she disappeared with her plane. Her disappearance is still one of aviation's greatest mysteries today.

The First U.S. Commercial Airplanes

As 1930 approached, most major cities in the United States established public spaces for airplanes called **municipal** airports. Later, construction programs improved and built additional airfields. All-weather paved runways would soon replace sod and bumpy, dirt landing areas. The government provided money to help build major airfields, early **control towers**, and radio equipment to a workable **air traffic control system**. The stage was set for the modern airliner.

 *Did you know?*

Many historical airplane builders, or manufacturers, don't exist anymore. They either combined with other companies or went out of business. There are well over a hundred aircraft manufacturers in the United States today. Some of them you should be familiar with. These include:

Boeing	Raytheon Company
General Dynamics Corporation	BAE Systems
Lockheed Martin Corporation,	Bombardier, Inc.
Northrop Grumman Corporation	

Around this time, the U.S. Post Office offered different types of pay for different aircraft mail carriers. For example, if an airplane could carry passengers along with the mail, it made more money, and that meant higher pay for the pilot.

Engineers hurried to design larger aircraft which led to the creation of the **Ford Tri-Motor.** It is known as one of the first cabin class airplanes, which meant it had a cabin, or space, for passengers to sit during the flight. It was called a "tri-motor" because it had three engines, which made it safer in case an engine lost power during flight.

The **Ford Tri-Motor** lost its popularity in 1931, after a terrible accident killed famous football coach **Knute Rockne**, from the University of Notre Dame. The wooden wing spars were blamed as a weakness in the structure. Engineers hurried to create something safer and bigger.

The idea that airplanes could have special space for paying passengers fueled the competition to build more that were bigger, faster, and, most importantly, safer. Because of this, another leap forward in airplane design was the creation of the **Boeing Company Model 247** in 1933. This airplane was built with two super-powerful 550 horsepower engines and retractable gear, which meant the landing wheels could be tucked up inside the plane during flight. It could travel 180 miles an hour and seat 10 passengers.

 ***Fast Fact***

On October 10th, 1933, a Boeing 247 exploded over Chesterton, Indiana. This accident is believed to have inspired the idea that aircraft could be used as weapons, like during World War II by Japanese suicide pilots.

The popularity of the **Boeing 247** was surpassed by the development of the DC-2 airplane. This design by the **Douglas Aircraft Company** had two, or "twin," all-metal engines and could fit 14 passengers. By 1936, the **DC-3** flew 185 miles an hour and seated 21 passengers. It became the most dependable commercial plane of its time, providing the transportation of 90 percent of the world's air traffic.

Across the Seas

The next challenge on the horizon would be to transport paying passengers across the oceans. In the late 1930s, aircraft manufacturers like Boeing and the **Martin Company** were building planes called "**flying boats**." These aircraft came with four engines that could transport passengers across the Atlantic or Pacific. They had boat-like **hulls** and could land and takeoff from water. However, they couldn't transfer large groups of passengers.

Many people believed that giant gas-filled **airships** were the answer. Germany developed an airship called a **Zeppelin**. It was a giant balloon that flew because of large bags filled with gases lighter than air. Gases like helium and hydrogen were used, but they were both flammable.

For more than 2,000 flights, thousands of people traveled by airship until 1937. Passengers had enjoyed travel on them between Europe, North America, and South America, with modern rooms, lounges, and a dining room On May 6, 1937, the German Zeppelin, *Hindenburg*, burst into flames and crashed in New Jersey. The disaster happened in a matter of seconds, killing 36 people and a man on the ground. It was caught on film by newsreel cameras on site to record the landing.

 ### *Fast Fact*

The original flying boats were designed by Russian-born American engineer, Igor Sikorsky. The Pan Am Company operated them overwater in the Caribbean region. This saved weeks of travel time compared with steamship and awkward railway connections.

During 1935, **Pan Am** completed the construction of many mid-ocean stop service locations on islands strung across the Pacific. The airline also installed its own radio communications and **meteorological**, or weather, network. Using flying boats, most of the early Pan Am flights across the Pacific carried mail, along with an occasional government or business passenger who could afford the high fares. In 1939, the new, imposing **Boeing 314** began scheduled airmail and luxury passenger service across the Atlantic to Europe.

All About Speed

With the oceans conquered, the airline industry in the United States turned to connecting large and small cities together as the country's population grew. In those early years, speed was more important to the engineers than the comfort of the passengers on board. The passengers did not have the luxuries we have today like comfortable seats, air conditioning, cool movies, internet access, and full size meals.

During the 1940s, Boeing introduced the pressurized **Stratoliner**. Pressurized means that the inside of the aircraft was filled with conditioned air, which allowed airplanes to fly high above bad weather. This helped flights leave and arrive on time, which improved schedules. It also gave passengers a more comfortable ride. Also, flying at higher altitudes increased fuel efficiency, meaning the plane could fly further.

To compete with Boeing, Douglas introduced the **DC-4.** Although it wasn't pressurized, it performed just as well and carried more passengers. One interesting change with the DC-4 was that it had a tricycle-type landing gear instead of one tail-wheel in the rear of the aircraft and two main landing gear located toward the front end. This change actually improved takeoff performance for the plane and the pilot.

The War

World War II slowed production of Boeing's Stratoliners and Douglas' DC-4 for passenger travel. Boeing began building bombers. The DC-4 was built during the war but was called the C-54. The U.S. Army Air Corps used it as its main transportation for long distances. Later in the war, a company called **Lockheed** created the **L-1049** Constellation with triple **vertical fins** to perform the same job.

After the war, many United States airlines looked for planes to use on shorter flights. The **Consolidated Vultee Aircraft Corporation** built the **Convair**. This popular plane was a twin-engine aircraft. More than 1,000 models were built between 1947 and 1956. Convairs could cruise at 280 miles per hour. Their pressurized cabin could provide comfort for 40 to 50 passengers depending on the model. Later copies of the Convair kept the type in service for several decades.

The Golden Age of Travel

After 1945, American aircraft manufacturers challenged one another to improve their products. North America's market for airliners kept companies busy, building plane after plane. This made the costs low and created jobs. Eventually, American designs dominated airline fleets around the world.

 *Fast Fact*

The 1950s is considered to be the Golden Age of air travel although it was very expensive. In 1955, a ticket from Chicago, Illinois, to Phoenix, Arizona, and back cost $130. That equals over $1,100 today.[2]

Boeing wanted to be the leader in aviation. To keep up with other aircraft companies, Boeing created the **Stratocruiser**. It offered unique luxury for air travelers in the late 1940s and early 50s. Its large cabin seated 55 passengers, and it had a spiral staircase and lounge. The Pan Am airline used Stratocruisers on its popular routes across the North Atlantic. Eventually, though, even this model lost its popularity with the creation of faster **piston-engine** airliners from Douglas and Lockheed.

---

2. Brownlee, 2013

There was still a remaining challenge during this era that was solved by the "**Seven Seas**." Coast to coast flights, called **transcontinental** flights, required stopping during the route to refuel. During the 1950s, improvements with the Lockheed **Super Constellation** and the **DC-7** made longer direct flights possible. The final model of the DC-7 appeared between 1956 and 1957. It was known as the DC-7C, or "Seven Seas," by those who flew it, because it could fly nonstop across the Atlantic.

The *Seven Seas* was capable of nonstop transatlantic flights in either direction. Its competitor, the **Lockheed 1649A Starliner,** could fly nonstop from Los Angeles to Europe. It held 75 passengers and cruised at speeds up to 400 miles per hour! These workhorse aircraft changed the world of air travel and remained in service with major airlines late into the 1960s.

Into the Future

The 1960s was a time of hippies and freedom marches. There was great civil change, but there were also two more important stages of aircraft development you should know. First, was the adoption of the **turbofan** engine. A turbofan engine is surrounded by a fan in the front and a **turbine** at the back.

The second achievement was the invention of a wider aircraft; the **Boeing 747**. It could seat 400 people. That was enormous for its time. Several more models were developed by Boeing during the 1960s that were created for specific routes.

 ***Fast Fact***

The most produced Boeing airplane in history is the 737 with more than 6,000 sales to different airlines.

During Boeing's expansion in the 1960s, the Douglas Company had problems. While its **DC-9** was a success, they were unable to match Boeing's explosion of new designs. The **McDonnell Aircraft Corporation** acquired Douglas in 1967. The new McDonnell Douglas Corporation produced a tri-motored **DC-10** to meet an estimated market requirement for about 750 wide-body, fuel-efficient aircraft.

Other companies tried to enter the same market but lost money. McDonnell Douglas hung on with an improved DC-10. They continued producing the DC-9, MD-80 and MD-90 series, until Boeing acquired the firm in 1997.

 ***Did you know?***

There are thousands of airlines operating around the world. Almost more than one can imagine! Of the major airlines, three fly throughout Africa and the Middle East. 25 fly across Asia and the Pacific. Over 15 serve Europe, and there are five in the Caribbean and Latin America. Do you recognize these airlines that originate from North America?

Air Canada	Delta Air Lines	SkyWest Airlines
AirTran Airways	ExpressJet Airlines	Southwest Airlines
Alaska Airlines	Frontier Airlines	United Airlines
American Airlines	JetBlue Airway	US Airways
American Eagle	Mesa Airlines	WestJet
Atlantic Southeast Airlines	Pinnacle Airlines	

In spite of all the competition to build airliners, a new challenger did appear in the early 1970s. **Airbus Industries** was co-owned by French, German, British, Spanish, Dutch, and Belgium companies. No one believed a new company could compete, but its aircraft lineup became widely accepted. United States aircraft manufacturers accused Airbus of being funded by various European governments.

The important thing to know about the Airbus Company is that it was the first manufacturer to introduce **fly-by-wire** technology with the **A-320**. The first digital fly-by-wire concept was in use as early as 1969 on the Lunar Module that landed on the moon. It meant that flight control laws, called **algorithms**, changed pilot control inputs into a code that activated computer operated aircraft systems. The majority of levers, cables, push rods, and pulleys to connect the pilot's controls to the airplane were no longer needed. This type of aircraft control was a first for commercial aviation. It is now the gold standard of aircraft control.

Because of all of the new technology, the first A-320 pilots were tested on just about everything. No one knew for sure what knowledge was needed and what was not necessary to pilot one of these modern marvels. Just because you can fly an airplane doesn't mean you have to know how to build one. Those "know everything" days are thankfully behind us. The human brain is amazing, but it's no match for the unbiased reasoning of a well-programmed computer.

Nearly a century has passed since the first airmail flights evolved into computer-operated airliners. What lies beyond the horizon is anyone's guess. The limits on aircraft speed and capacity today are both technical and psychological. How big is too big, and how fast is too fast? We are at a new dawn in air travel.

CHAPTER 3

So You Want to Be a Pilot

Like most careers, becoming a pilot is a series of steps that lead up a staircase to success that takes years to achieve. Education comes first. It's likely a pilot or flight attendant will spend nearly half their working life away from home pursuing this career, so there is much preparation.

 ***Fast Fact***

The path to becoming a pilot is not the same for everyone, although everyone needs the same pilot certificates.

Typically a future commercial pilot will learn to fly, instruct, serve as a **first officer**, and eventually become a captain. Of course, the first step is to actually learn to fly an airplane and earn a series of certificates called airman certificates. These basic certificates are the **Private, Instrument, Commercial, and Flight Instructor** certificates. A Flight Instructor certificate is not required, but it helps a pilot build up flight time teaching students.

From the cockpit

"I honestly wasn't considering being a pilot because my vision wasn't very good. I wore a strong prescription in my glasses and contacts that enabled me to see 20/20, but I didn't know if that would keep me from being hired. With some encouragement from others, I looked into aviation a little more seriously and found out my school had an aviation program that had just started one year earlier. I went and talked to a few people in the department and decided to give it a go! My years in the university program consisted of getting my four year degree in aviation (Your degree can be in anything) and earning my pilot's licenses at my local airport." ■

The Private certificate is just like a driver's license. It makes it legal for you to fly, with passengers, anywhere in the United States. Flying with only a private license allows you to fly up to 18,000 feet, but you are not allowed to fly into the clouds.

The Instrument certificate is required to show a pilot can fly using only instruments in the cockpit. Today, a person who applies for this instrument rating must have a private pilot license, have logged 50 hours of cross-country flight time, 40 hours of instrument time, and 15 hours of instrument instruction from an authorized trainer.

The Commercial certificate is one of the most important certificates you will ever earn. It allows you to be paid for flight. A commercial pilot today must be at least 18 years old, speak English, hold a special medical certificate, have a private pilot license, and log 250 hours of flight time. Also, to earn the commercial certificate, several challenging written exams must be passed.

The Flight Instructor certificate comes after the Commercial certificate. It requires a Commercial certificate and a series of tests. These tests are the Fundamentals of Instructing (FOI), the Flight Instructor FAA Knowledge Test, and a verbal examination and flight test.

You can find all of the requirements for the certificates you need at the Aircraft Owners and Pilots Association at https://www.aopa.org/.

From the cockpit

"After I got out of the Army, I applied and was accepted at Embry-Riddle Aeronautical University in Daytona Beach, Florida. I went full time including summers and finished my B.S. degree in Aeronautical Science, and completed my commercial pilot's license, instrument rating, multi-engine rating, and flight instructor's certificate there." ∎

The basic job requirements for most major airlines are shown below:

- At least 23 years of age.

- Graduate of a four-year degree program accredited by a U.S. Department of Education recognized accrediting organization

- Current passport or other travel documents

- Eligible to work in the United States

FAA Requirements

- FAA Commercial Fixed-Wing Pilot license with Instrument Rating

- Current FAA First Class Medical Certificate

- Successful completion of Airline Transport Pilot (ATP) written test

Flight Time Requirements

- Minimum of 1,500 hours of total documented flight time

- Minimum of 1,000 hours of fixed-wing turboprop or turbofan time flight time

Other Requirements

- Must provide appropriate documentation [to support] all flight hours and college transcripts

- FCC Radiotelephone Operators Permit (RP)

- Department of Transportation (DOT) required pre-employment drug test

- Transportation Security Administration (TSA) fingerprint for criminal history records check

- Company background check

From A to B

There are two ways to learn to fly. You can start with flying lessons to earn your certificates. Plan on it adding up to about 250 hours of flight time with a price tag around $35,000 to earn a commercial certificate with instrument, multi-engine, and instructor licenses. Every time you fly an airplane, you will record, or "log" how much time you spent in the sky in a journal called a logbook. Once you are qualified to work as a flight instructor, you can teach students to fly to gain the approximate 750 hours you need to apply for an entry-level commercial airline job. Flight instructors can make up to $25 an hour, and you will learn a lot about flying by watching and teaching others.

From the cockpit

"After school, I didn't have enough experience to be hired as a commercial airline pilot, so I started work as a flight instructor in Idaho Falls, Idaho. I taught for just over a year before I built enough time to be hired by a regional airline flying a 50-passenger regional jet." ∎

A second way for both men and women to learn to fly is joining the military. A four year college degree allows you to apply for flight training in one of the branches of the Armed Forces. This is a six-to-eight year commitment, but after the military, you can apply as a commercial pilot with an airline and expect to be a top candidate.

From the cockpit

"I set a goal of becoming an astronaut, so my focus became centered on a military career. At the time, there was a seven-year commitment to the Navy after you got winged." ∎

A Commercial Airline Pilot Career Path

Year 2-3

Work as a flight instructor.

- Log 750 hours of additional flight time
- Earn $5-25 per hour

Year 1

Acquire Private, Instrument, Commercial, and Flight Instructor Certificates.

- 250 hours of flight
- $35,000 in 2015 dollars

Alternate:

- Military flight training
- 6 to 8 year commitment

Job 4

- Acquire 7 - 16 years of seniority
- Apply to major airline as Captain
- Earn $100,000 -$200,000 per year

Job 3

- 3,000 – 5,000 hours of flight time
- Apply to major airline as First Officer
- Earn $40,000 - $50,000 the first year.

Job 2

- Obtain Airline Transport Pilot (ATP) certificate at own expense
- 1,500 logged hours of flight
- Apply as Regional airline captain
- Earn $45,000 the first year

Job 1

- 1,000 hours
- Apply for regional airline First Officer
- Earn $16,000 - $20,000 the first year

On The Job Training

After you have logged, or recorded, at least 1,000 hours in the air, you are ready to apply for a commercial airline pilot position. Your first job as a pilot will prepare you for someday becoming the captain of a great passenger airliner. Commercial pilots often begin in smaller planes, usually at a **regional** airline, that only flies from city to city within a state or from one state to another close by. Regional jets usually have between 50 and 100 seats.

 ***Fast Fact***

An example of a popular regional jet that carries small groups of passengers is the CRJ, or officially known as the Bombardier CRJ100/200.

When they are first hired, new pilots are usually First Officers. They are often put on "**reserve**." This means they usually have to wait for a call to report to work — sometimes with only an hour notice. It's kind of like being a substitute teacher. Being on reserve might waste 20 to 22 days a month. Depending on the need for reserves, reserve pilots might not fly at all during the month, but they're still tied to the telephone.

The next stair step in your career will be to upgrade to the position of captain with the regional airline. This takes time, at least three years or so. As captain, and even as a first officer for some airlines, you are required to have the most important document: the **Airline Transport Pilot Certificate**. To earn this certificate, a pilot must have 1,500 flight hours and be prepared to pay several thousands of dollars to get it.

As captain for a regional airline, you will add even more hours of flight to your logbook. Typically a captain of a smaller airplane will log at least 800-

1,000 hours a year as the Pilot-in-Command. The goal is to log and prove you have between 3,000 and 5,000 hours flying aircraft before applying to a major airline with large airplanes. Plan on spending 3-5 years at the regionals before making the move to your dream job.

From the cockpit

"There was a small company in Memphis that was just getting started where I could get my Airline Transport Pilot certificate and a rating in a Falcon 20 (jet). I applied and was accepted into their program. After I completed the program and received my ATP, they offered me a job which I immediately accepted. The startup company was Federal Express, which later became FEDEX. I spent the next 37 years with FEDEX." ■

After working for a few years flying for regional airline companies, the day will come when you can fly a bigger aircraft for a major airline as a first officer. This is a crucial achievement in your career, because it can take up to 20 years of flight experience in different types of airplanes and in all kinds of conditions before you can captain a major airliner.

A first officer at a major airline can expect to see their pay increase to around $50,000 in the second year. Unless the airline is new or quite young, there will be thousands of pilots ahead of you on a **seniority** list. A seniority list is a record of the company's pilots and what day they were hired. Becoming a captain means waiting in line until you move up to about the middle of the seniority list. This can take up to 15 years depending on the number of people above you on the list and the rate of retirement by senior captains. This is not wasted time. Serving as a first officer will train and prepare you for what's to come.

It's important to understand that a large number of pilots come from the military. Their training, in most cases, cost the government over a million dollars. Many of these pilots have flown almost to the edge of space and some have actually orbited Earth. Even with all this experience, even the astronauts start at the bottom of the airline seniority list.

It's not uncommon for junior captains at smaller airlines to have less experience than military-trained First or Second Officers. However, over time it usually becomes meaningless; with rare exception, the person in the captain's seat is usually the most qualified pilot.

 ***Fast Fact***

An airline captain wears four stripes on each sleeve.

No airline captain earns their stripes because they have brilliant flying skills, mad courage, or good looks. They have endured many years of flying as a first officer and waiting for their names to rise to the top of the seniority list. However, before you know it, you will earn your captain's stripes at last.

As a major airline pilot, your income will change dramatically. You can expect to earn well over a hundred thousand dollars a year. Becoming the captain of an enormous jumbo jet, you will be at the peak of your career after patiently enduring the long climb up, constant education, training, and a long seniority list.

Probation and More Tests

New hires with major airlines are usually put on probation, or a trial period for their first year of employment. During that time, those without the "right stuff" are usually fired. It's a brutal time. Probation is an unavoidable fact of life when starting your career with an airline. In that first year, no one cares if you have 10,000 hours of military flying, commercial flying, a lunar landing, or only a few thousand hours of private flight time. Probation pilots are treated all the same.

All major United States' airlines have, as a condition of continued employment, the ability to terminate your job for little or no reason in the first year of your job. During probation, you can be let go at any time based on a single incident.

From the cockpit

"Normally, the company does not want to terminate anyone, since by hiring them they've invested a lot in them. However, there may be occasions where a pilot may not be able to pass the checks or may not get along with other crew members, and they may be terminated." ∎

Probation is a trial period. It affords both pilot and the employer an opportunity to spend time together, testing their compatibility. Because the grievance, or complaint, procedures don't apply during this first year, the airline can end the relationship without worrying about any contract agreements. Pilot contracts (agreements) often require lengthy grievance procedures that must be carried out before a pilot can be terminated.

Throughout the first year of a pilot's employment on probation, he or she will likely fly with dozens of different captains. Each of these captains may be asked for a written review of the new pilot's performance on the job. These reviews typically go to the chief pilot's office where the pilot is assigned. Several times during the first year the probation pilot is called into the chief pilot's office for a review of their performance.

 **_Fast Fact_**

The evaluation report is typically a form filled with questions on timeliness, attention to detail, preparedness, and piloting skills. To make things easier for the captain, they are usually answered by checkmarks in satisfactory or unsatisfactory boxes. The pilot on probation is often the one who actually hands the form to the captain. Talk about nerves!

Typically new pilots are required to turn in at least one evaluation form each month. As one would expect, some new hires make sure all is going well between them and their captain before asking them to fill out an evaluation form. Some captains treat this lightly, but most are very serious about the process.

Airlines hire pilots because they need them. The odds favor the survival of the probation year, but it's still uncomfortable knowing you're being closely watched. From the second year until the time a pilot checks out as a captain, the career of a commercial airline pilot can be a roller coaster ride.

Some pilots choose to stay on the same piece of equipment, or plane, they flew on probation until they can upgrade. This is the easy path and requires less strain on both the pilot and their family.

Others "chase the bucks" and bigger airplanes. This means a pilot will move anywhere to fly larger planes and make more money. Larger equipment usually pays more per hour, but each time a pilot upgrades, there is a lengthy and technically difficult education. This can put your job or ability to move up in the future at risk if you fail to complete the upgrade training. Learning to fly a new and bigger airplane at this level of an aviation career is not as easy as one might think, so some pilots avoid that risk by staying where they are.

Check Rides

During your career as a pilot, you will often be required to take tests called **Check Rides**. Each year as a first officer and each six months as a captain requires a check ride. It is also required that you pass a verbal or written exam on the airplane and the company's flight operation procedures. To make it as close to real life as possible, check rides are usually given in a computer **simulator** that mirrors actual situations.

From the cockpit

There was a typical drinking-from-a-fire-hose approach, where they crammed as much information down our throats as we could handle. After that, we entered simulator training, where I begin to actually learn how to fly the aircraft, talk on the radios, and otherwise manage the flight routine. Once those steps were complete, we began the actual aircraft flying. ∎

An airline pilot in a 30-year career can expect to have around 50 such check rides, maybe more. These testing periods are not a walk in the park, but some pilots say they enjoy the challenge of having their skills tested. Of course, they are always relieved when the check ride is over!

 ***Fast Fact***

A typical aircraft operating manual is as thick as a college textbook.

To prepare for tests and check rides, more studying and exams are required. Two-to six-week classes take you through the aircraft's systems, but the trend today is for pilots to use electronic media to essentially teach themselves all about the new aircraft before they show up for class. Remember, a jet, is a jet, is a jet. Unfortunately, though they fly alike, all jets are not built alike.

So, if a jet is a jet, what's the big deal about checking out in one? The Boeing 777 has a lot of switches, push buttons, and warning lights. For the captain to receive what is called a **type rating** in this plane, he or she must demonstrate a working knowledge of each and every control in the cockpit from memory. It requires hours and hours of study to have a basic mastery of a modern jet. Fortunately, most airlines have developed a building block technique when it comes to airplane instruction.

 ***Fast Fact***

A type rating is a printed endorsement on your airman certificate, or approval, that proves a pilot is qualified to be a captain on a specific type of aircraft.

The classes

Usually weeks or months before any training for a new aircraft begins, airplane manuals and electronic media like DVDs and CDs are issued. That way the pilot can read and study to get ahead before the actual first day of what they call **ground school**. This shifts some of the cost of training to the pilot by reducing time the pilot has to spend at the airline's training facility.

After weeks of ground school and hundreds of study hours, you are given an in depth "must pass" test requiring you correctly answer 90 percent of the aircraft systems questions. Captains must then pass an FAA verbal test, and first officers must pass one given by one of the airline's instructor pilots. The captain will be acquiring the all-important type rating. It's important to understand that a first officer is not normally "typed." That's why a verbal test from the FAA is not required.

 ***Fast Fact***

Some airlines now require pilots to show up the first day of training and take a "must pass" airplane systems test.

The second step of a check ride is full-motion simulator training. This means there will be computer simulation tests. Since computers are playing a larger role in flying aircraft, pilots are slowly becoming computer managers. Because computers can now fly planes, a modern autopilot paired up with what is called a **flight management guidance computer** (FMGC) is a marvelous bit of technology. A pilot only has to type in a flight plan, get airborne, and engage the autopilot. A modern day airliner can take passengers all the way from one runway to touchdown at another destination. This is both good and bad. Automated flight is so common that some pilots complain they're losing their mechanical flying skills.

 ***From the cockpit***

"The longest captain verbal [exam] I ever had, was when I checked out as a Boeing 727 captain. It was almost seven hours." ■

For testing purposes, the computerized airplane-training simulator is a marvelous creation. Prior to computer simulators, all of a pilot's airplane training was accomplished in the actual plane. Usually, the pilot would have to pick up the airplane after it had finished with the day's passenger flying. It was usually at night. Considered glorious days by yesterday's pilots, that kind of real training meant boring holes through the sky, practicing runway approach after runway approach, and dealing with pretend fires and engine failures. Talk about reality! It was risky, costly, and sometimes even deadly.

Simulators now play a vital role in assuring the paying passenger that their crew has been exposed to inflight emergencies that could never be simulated safely in a real airplane without endangering crew or aircraft. Today's simulators are so lifelike in their performance and in the appearance of an aircraft's interior that after an hour it's hard to remember you're in a box inside a building.

Before entering the simulator for a training session, a meeting, called a briefing, covers all details of that training period and can last as long as two hours.

During flight simulation, the instructor sits behind the pilots at a panel that controls almost every indication light or button available.

Once in the "box" or the simulator, the period usually starts with a cockpit preflight reading of the checklist, and then it's followed by a takeoff and climb-out checklist. That's when everything goes crazy. One failure after another is introduced, and the crew has to work the problem as if they are actually flying a scheduled trip.

The visuals out of the simulator's cockpit windows are computer generated, but very realistic. For the next two to three hours, a pilot will fight engine fires, engine losses, depressurization, **hydraulic** failures, navigation failures, bad weather, passenger medical emergencies, and even an airplane evacuation.

Besides working the problem, the pilot is still expected to make calls to air traffic control, inform the passengers and **flight attendants**, and reprogram computers, all while controlling the airplane and trying to resolve the problem using a lengthy and complex checklist.

The type rating check ride is the finale to your training as a captain on a new jet. You've been exposed to major emergencies involving every system on the airplane. The verbal exams are behind you, but they were only half of the check ride. Once you enter the simulator you're to treat everything as though you were on a real flight in a real airplane. You cannot ask for any help other than what you might access in the real world.

 **_Did you know?_**

Learning how to fly a new jet airliner has been likened to getting a Ph.D. in 45 days. You won't need to write a big research paper, but you will just about need to recite one from memory at the end of your training. Additionally, there are the verbal exams that last for hours, and finally, the simulator check ride, which may leave permanent sweat stains on your clothing!

These simulation periods are anything but a joy ride. Even instructors who've worked in simulators for years say they learn as much from watching others as they taught them. At times, the drama of these simulations becomes so intense that everyone forgets it's all just pretend!

Failing a type rating check ride at this level is embarrassing for the pilot, and for the airline it is an undesired expense. Some airlines have a "two-failures-and-you're fired policy." Check rides are serious business.

In addition to re-occurring check rides as often as twice a year, pilots are checked periodically without notice during actual flights. For these tests, a **check airman**, who is a captain from the training department, watches you from a cockpit **jump seat** as you fly a leg of your trip. All of these check rides may seem daunting, but it's all part of the job.

Paychecks and Rewards

You will not make a great deal of money when you first become a pilot and are able to flight instruct other students in small aircraft. Once you take the next step and become a First Officer at a regional airline, the money will get a little better.

 **_Fast Fact_**

A new commercial pilot for a regional airline could earn between $16,000 and $20,000 a year for the first year. The poverty line, a government standard that identifies the poor working class, was estimated to be $16,000 a year for two people in 2017. You may need an extra job on the side!

Once you become a captain at a small regional airline, the pay increases. You can expect to earn enough to make life easier as you wait until you have enough logged hours to apply to a major airline. After several years, chances are good that you'll be able to acquire a job as a first officer at a major airline. When that time comes, you can expect your pay to start at around $50,000 a year. It will be a big change from your days as a first officer on a regional jet making less than half of that.

The day you earn your Captain's stripes, you will finally be able to have the generous income that you have worked so long and hard for. Captains of major airlines earn between $100,000 and $250,000 per year. Not only that, they are only required to work between 75 and 90 hours a month, depending on the airline. The job starts when the airplane backs out of the gate at one airport and ends when they set the brakes and park at the gate of the next airport.

Unfortunately, pilots spend a great deal of time at work not getting paid. Remember they only get paid for the time they are actually taxiing or flying. This means they are not getting paid while passengers are getting on or off the aircraft.

The eventual high pay is a nice reward for those the years of hard work. Many people believe pilots earn too much money. However, a pilot that flies for an average of 30 years will be on the job 27,000 hours longer than people in other careers.

 **Fast Fact**

One retired pilot noted in 20 years of working as a captain, he actually worked 58 hours for each 20 hours of pay.

Not all captains make the same amount of money. The only way a pilot gets a pay raise is to move to a larger airplane once they reach the top pay for their current plane. This usually takes 10 to 12 years, but it's worth it.

Rewards

It's true. An airline captain's job begins with low wages. There are long years of training as a first officer. Then, for many pilots, there are life and family challenges that come from being on the road half of an employee's life. In 35 years of airline flying, one pilot counted that he had spent only eight Christmas days and three of his birthdays at home. The rest of any other celebrations were spent with crewmembers, flying a trip.

 **From the cockpit**

"A good day is a flight "to Cancun with a 48-hour layover!" ∎

Although they are gone from home a lot, pilots have amazing opportunities to travel and meet new people. Besides the good pay, they can take cool vacations. Pilots are able to fly free on the airline they work for to almost anywhere in the world. They can get discounts on other airlines their company may be associated with. Also, they get to take their families with them for free or a small service charge!

Pilots get to meet all kinds of people. Many pilots find their future husbands or wives at work. Sometimes, they have the opportunity to fly famous people like professional football, basketball, and hockey players, not to mention many politicians and movie celebrities. If that's not nice enough, there are large yearly bonuses with some airlines as well as wealthy retirement plans for the future.

From the cockpit

"When I was 14, my Sunday School teacher at church had just moved into our area. He was an awesome teacher and he happened to have a Porsche 911, which to a 14-year-old boy, was pretty cool! He also happened to work as a pilot." ■

Remember, becoming a pilot takes time. It may be one of the most risky jobs in the world, but it does come with a great salary and the most beautiful office view in the world.

 **Did you know?**

Airline pilots have a moral code'

The Airline Pilots Association (ALPA) has a code of ethics, **or** morals and beliefs, about how someone should conduct himself or herself as an airline pilot. The Code of Ethics states that pilots will think of the safety and comfort of passengers as highly as possible because they are putting their trust in him or her.

A pilot should also accept full responsibility as well as the rewards of flying an aircraft. He or she will act with confidence and do everything possible to earn the respect of others both on and off duty.

The Code of Ethics also reminds a pilot that everything he or she does brings honor or dishonor upon the piloting profession. He or she will be a law-abiding citizen and do everything possible to become the safest, more knowledgeable, and best pilot one can be.

You can read the full ALPA Code of Ethics at: **http://www.alpa.org/en/about-alpa/what-we-do/code-of-ethics.**

CHAPTER 4

A Typical Day

Once passenger boarding is complete and the cockpit door closes, things get busy for airline pilots. Of course, a typical day begins much earlier once a captain and crew arrive at the airport one hour before the plane departs.

Pilots review the weather, fuel requirements for the trip, and their flight plans when they first get to work. Most of these reviews are done once they're onboard the airplane. For long or international flights across the sea, there are often times special rooms in the airport for working on flight plans and crew meetings.

The pilots also check out the plane they will fly that day, both inside and out. The FAA requires that a cockpit crewmember walk around the aircraft before each and every flight. Not all gates where the airplane is parked have mechanics standing by, so a pilots' outside pre-flight examination bridges the inspection gap. This inspection is generally referred to as "a walk-around." Of course, mechanics usually give a better pre-flight inspection. This is why a certified mechanic will do a complete aircraft pre-flight at least once each day the aircraft is in service.

Pilots performing a walk-around look for obvious things on their inspections: fuel or oil leaks, airframe and tire conditions, and anything out of the ordinary. It's a good system that has saved airlines from many tragic situations. It also gives the pilot a chance to stretch his or her legs and listen to the roar of the jet engines. Pilots say they love the smell of jet fuel in the morning!

From the cockpit

"A typical day is waking up in a hotel when it's dark and waiting for a ride to the airport. You get through security screening and hurry to your gate. If you're real early, the restaurants in the terminal are closed. You fly to your first destination and hope for a cup of coffee from a flight attendant. You land, say good-bye to the passengers, and get ready for the next flight. After a long day you head to the overnight hotel for a short sleep, then the whole process starts all over again." ∎

As departure time nears, both the captain and first officer run down different checklists. The captain is now the ringleader for a show that can have many endings, so the cockpit becomes serious and quiet. If the captain's directions are professional, the flight will be safe and flawless. If an error is made, the consequences can sometimes be disastrous.

In 1981, the FAA imposed the **Sterile Cockpit Rule** as a result of several crashes where crews were distracted from their jobs by unimportant conversations and activities during critical parts of the flight below 10,000 feet.

There are lots of distractions beneath the 10,000-foot mark in the sky. Once in the air, pilots spend most of their time watching the airplane systems, getting requests from flight attendants, and re-calculating the estimate of the future arrival time for the company. There aren't many chances to look outside the window for traffic.

Here are some things a captain deals with once the cockpit is sterile and preparations are made for engine start and takeoff. At the same time, the first officer is equally as busy.

- Verify air traffic control clearance.

- Direct first officer to call for **pushback clearance** to back away from the gate.

- Contact the pushback crew working around the plane while monitoring a frequency for changes in the "push" clearance.

- When cleared by pushback crew, start the engines call for an engine start checklist.

- Command and monitor the engine start while making sure the pushback crew is following directions given by ramp control.

- Once one engine is started and the pushback crew has requested "Brakes set – are we cleared to disconnect?" the captain sets the brakes and clears the "push" crew to disconnect from the aircraft.

- Call for a **Before Taxi Check**.

- Before taxi check is complete, request first officer to obtain the taxi clearance.

After an often complex taxiway route is issued by ground control, both the captain and first officer confirm the route by looking at a taxiway diagram. It's a small map with lots of details. Taxiways are named by the alphabet or alpha-numerically like A-1 or B-2. They are pronounced using the **Phonetic Alphabet** where A-1 is pronounced "Alpha 1," and B-2 is pronounced "Bravo 2" and so on.

At last, the airplane begins to move under its own power.

 ***Fast Fact***

Pilots and others in aviation use the Phonetic Alphabet to communicate clearly. This language uses a word for each letter of the alphabet. For example, instead of saying, "B-2" to a pilot, an air traffic controller would say "Bravo-2."

A - Alpha	J - Juliet	S - Sierra
B - Bravo	K - Kilo	T - Tango
C - Charlie	L - Lima	U - Uniform
D - Delta	M - Mike	V - Victor
E - Echo	N - November	W - Whiskey
F - Foxtrot	O - Oscar	X - X-ray
G - Golf	P - Papa	Y - Yankee
H - Hotel	Q - Quebec	Z - Zulu
I - India	R - Romeo	

Moving down a taxiway is like rolling down an enormous highway. The captain can't see the plane's wing tips or tail, so the taxi is a deliberate slow ride through crowded ramp and gate areas to avoid crashing into another aircraft or obstacle. This is harder than it sounds.

A Boeing 777 has a wingspan of almost 200 feet and a length of just over 242 feet. Following painted center lines on a taxiway is the safest way of making sure the plane stays on the pavement. When there is snow on the ground a jumbo jet needs to stay on the taxiway centerlines even though they can be difficult to see. Running off the taxiway or cutting the corner too sharp can cause a costly traffic jam, not to mention delays.

Taxiing can be even more challenging when the captain is responding to a checklist. It's a bit like texting and driving (which is illegal and incredibly dangerous while driving a car.) In an airplane it's legal, but it can be a bit unnerving for the pilot.

Once the airplane is the first aircraft in line to take off, there is still another checklist. The air traffic controllers clear the plane for takeoff. The pilot that will fly assumes control of the aircraft. This control is usually swapped between the captain and first officer on different trips to make sure both pilots stay skilled.

What if things go wrong? Many people don't know the captain is the only one that can abort the takeoff prior to a **decision speed,** or the absolute speed limit up to which a captain can change their mind and bring the aircraft to a dramatic stop on the runway. The captain orchestrates everything that happens during an abort. In this happens, things move lightning fast. For example, if the air traffic control tower is not paying attention, someone could land on top of the plane after the abort. There is also a small chance that the tires might explode or the hot brakes catch the airplane on fire because of heat that builds up in the tires during the giant effort to stop. Of course, this is extremely rare. If that happens, the captain will broadcast "evacuate the aircraft" over the PA and an escape slide ride to the outside world will get you away from the airplane and other dangers.

 *Fast Fact*

The speed at takeoff depends on the plane and its overall takeoff weight. Most airliners are airborne between 130 to 160 miles an hour.

Assuming a takeoff is successful, you now climb "out" into the most crowded airspace in the sky. There are planes everywhere in the air around an airport. That's what the air traffic control tower on the ground is for.

First, the airplane is "cleaned up". This phrase means the gear (the wheels) and the flaps on the wings are **retracted**. Next, the aircraft accelerates to a cruising speed up to 250 **knots** (about 288 miles per hour). Once above

10,000 feet in the sky, the pilot can accelerate to the cruising speed, which can be as fast as 600 knots (690 miles per hour).

 ### *Fast Fact*

The standard speed limit for aircraft below 10,000 feet is 250 knots.

Even with an airliner equipped instrument system known as the **Traffic Collision Avoidance System (TCAS)** that warns the crew of an impending collision into other planes, both pilots watch carefully and constantly to avoid hitting other aircraft. The avoidance system helps, but it's not foolproof, especially around busy airport skies.

At last, above 10,000 feet, the captain turns off the sterile cockpit light in the main cabin. It is the first chime a passenger will hear once up in the air. This alerts flight attendants that they can now move around the cabin, and call or access the cockpit.

 ### *From the cockpit*

"Typically, the aircraft only talks to two control towers: one as they depart and one as they arrive. Right after speaking to the tower on departure, and long before talking to the new tower on arrival, they will talk to the TRACON (Terminal RADAR Approach Control). In-between the TRACONs, pilots talk to ARTCCs (Air Route Traffic Control Centers) along the way. During the entire flight, from one location to another, they are under the watchful eye of air traffic controllers."

The cockpit crew continues to navigate and monitor fuel consumption and aircraft systems while en route. They also get regular updates on the destination's weather. Regardless, once in the air, a pilot is doing what he loves to do: fly.

The Flight Crew

In a commercial aircraft there is a flight crew, also called an aircrew. There are positions, beginning with the captain, which are similar to the rank used in the military and at sea. Having structure makes it possible for the most senior and knowledgeable person to make a fast or final decision in an emergency.

 **Fast Fact**

You can tell who is captain and who is first officer by the uniform. The captain has four stripes on his coat or shirt. The first officer has three stripes. If there is a second officer, he or she has two stripes. Flight attendants have one stripe.

The aircrew is led by the captain, who is the Pilot-in-Command. He or she has the highest rank aboard the airplane. Next is the First Officer, often called the F/O, or co-pilot. The first officer sits in the right seat to the right of the captain. Both the captain and first officer take turns flying the aircraft.

 **From the cockpit**

"A good pilot knows the plane, takes initiative to get the job done, has a good attitude, shows up early, and most importantly stays ahead of the airplane while in flight." ∎

In the cockpit or resting in another part of the plane, may be a Second Officer. This position is sometimes called the Flight Engineer. In the distant past, the engineer worked the engines or managed the fuel, but today he or she (if qualified) may also help fly the plane when it's necessary for senior officers to rest on very long flights. Large aircraft have special bunks for the officers to sleep in when they are not at the controls.

From the cockpit

"On very long flights, especially overseas, there are usually two entire crews. Typically, one crew takes off and lands, and the other crew flies the middle of the trip. While one crew is flying, the other crew is resting or sleeping in the crew bunks." ■

Fast Fact

A nonstop flight from New York to Japan is about 14 hours long.

There are other cockpit positions from early aviation which are now outdated. If your grandfather flew during World War II, he may have been a navigator or radio operator.

Navigators could plot a course across land and sea using the horizon or stars. They were particularly helpful when the plane flew over oceans or other parts of the world where radio navigation did not work. Today, computers have replaced the job of the early navigators.

Aircrews also once had radio operators. Radio operators were in charge of the aircraft's communications. This meant talking on a radio or using a telegraph to communicate with stations set up from one location to the next. Again, technology advanced so far that pilots and other crewmembers could handle the radio communications. Radio operators aren't needed on a commercial aircraft anymore.

From the cockpit

"When you are flying with a crew, you are with them for the entire length of the trip. This could be one day or for as long as 11 days depending on what airplane you are on and how senior you are at your airline. The best trips are with pilots that are fun to talk to and have a positive energy around them." ■

There is another crew aboard a commercial aircraft outside the cockpit. Flight attendants play a crucial role for paying passengers. Flight attendants make up the cabin crew. Crewmembers that work in the aircraft cabin tend to the comfort, needs, or emergencies of the passengers. They help guests board, stow any belongings, find their seats, and understand any safety rules.

Airline companies today invest money and time into making sure the flight in the cabin is a calm and pleasant experience. Today, flight attendants serve refreshments, sell meals, and offer entertainment options like movies and internet service.

Historically, pilots were men and flight attendants were women. With progress and civil rights, things have changed. Today, all aircrew positions are available to anyone regardless of gender, race, or other differences. Flight attendants from different countries work on different airlines. Men and women from different countries all around the world fly and work together every day.

From the cockpit

"A good day is what makes this job the best job. They days where you arrive on time, have good weather and complimentary passengers, no maintenance, and good landings. Usually this also means you are at the hotel or home on time." ■

For a pilot, the ability to command an airline crew is far more difficult than most can imagine. In the fast-paced airline business, a crewmember bounces around different airplanes like a cue ball on a pool table. In fact, because of complicated resting rules and different schedules, it's not uncommon for cockpit and cabin crews to change several times during a series of trips. Each time a crewmember is added or taken away, the relationship, or vibe, of that particular crew changes.

Here's an example: Your start a trip with first officer who, like the captain, loves hunting. During the first three legs of the trip they get along great sharing stories during quiet moments. They work well as a cohesive team piloting the aircraft. Then, on the fifth leg of the trip, a new first officer replaces the hunter. Unfortunately, this officer hates guns and hunting. This changes the atmosphere in the cockpit. The changed feelings in the cockpit can affect the others working in the cabin.

From the cockpit

"I once worked with a pilot flying unstable approaches and who, in my opinion, was reckless. Various times I told him that I felt uncomfortable. He told me to shut up. We landed, and I threatened to walk off the airplane. He convinced me to fly back to the company hub where we could work things out. I flew, and he sat there. When we landed, he said, 'I'll be back.' He called in fatigued, and I never saw him again." ∎

A good captain seeks common ground to set the stage for a pleasant trip. A weak captain turns silent and makes the trip unbearable for everyone. To summarize, when a **flight deck crew** locks the cockpit door, the work environment becomes a tiny space where personality clashes have to be controlled. You can't just get up and walk away.

Schedules and Destinations

Work schedules in the airline industry are different from month to month. In the past, a pilot could choose to fly the same trip every month. Today, computer schedule planning technology helps plan trips to make them more efficient, so the departure times don't stay the same. They may shift forward an hour or back a day. This means the schedule for the pilot changes, even if it's the same route.

Airline crews bid schedules based on seniority. Those who worked for the company the longest claim the best schedules, which give them the best days off. The higher a pilot's seniority, the more options he or she has to choose from. There are different reasons for bidding on different schedules. Some pilots live far from the airport and like to get their flights done as days in a row each month. Other pilots like to spread days out. This is especially important when there are birthdays or special events pending.

From the cockpit

"As far as schedules go, my favorite trips left in the afternoon, spent the night in another city, and returned in the morning." ∎

The most senior pilots get to choose, or bid, on the schedules first. There are regular "lines" or schedules, and then there are the reserves.

A pilot with a line schedule is assigned duty in advance. About 14 days off are scheduled around trips throughout the month. They expect to work about 12 hours a day with 7 to 8 hours of actual flight time. A typical weekly schedule may be three days at work, then four days off.

A reserve schedule is usually for junior pilots. In an average month, there may be about 12 days off. However, on reserve days the pilot is on call. This means he or she might be called into work at the last minute or not at all.

From the cockpit

"I have spent many nights sleeping in crew rooms after a flight, usually by choice, lack of money, or because of late arrivals and missed commuter flights home. Honestly, I feel more at home sleeping in a dilapidated recliner than I do in my own bed, and I love vending machine food." ∎

Large planes that fly great distances in one trip mean the crew will stay at a hotel overnight. Smaller planes may do between five or six legs a day, and then the pilot either sleeps at a hotel or goes home if he or she is lucky.

Some pilots like short flights, while others love long haul overseas flying. Long-haul pilots usually make more money and have more days off. The downside is when they go to work, it can be for weeks at a time, and they are rarely in contact with their family.

Fast Fact

Depending on the schedule of a trip, you may arrive back home anywhere between one day to two weeks!

Another problem with long flights for a pilot is that he or she is halfway around the world. The body's natural defenses must get used to the time zone changes after a few days. That's mostly good. Unfortunately, when they return home, long haul pilots are on an opposite sleep schedule from the rest of their family. It takes several days to readjust back to the same sleep and wake periods. Then, about the time the pilot starts feeling normal again, it's time to go on another trip, and the off-schedule sleep pattern starts again.

This is bad for everyone's health and a real problem for some pilots. For men, it can cause a painful condition around the prostate gland and bladder called **prostatitis**. For women, and on rare occasions some men, it can cause **fibromyalgia**. Fibromyalgia is severe fatigue, aches, and pain.

From the cockpit

"It seemed like I was always sick when I flew the Boeing 747. I loved being on the plane, but the trips could be physically brutal, especially the west to east all-night crossings of the Pacific." ∎

Airline pilot duty days are much longer than a typical eight-hour work day in an office. When the time traveling back and forth to work is added in, a pilot might find the actual duty day can last over 20 hours. This is especially true 'if you are a long-haul pilot. It sounds like a model for disaster, but pilots do get used to it.

Destinations

There are about 87,000 flights a day in the United States alone.[3] That creates a great deal of available jobs for pilots who are ready to work. The top five airports with the highest traffic in the United States are in the big cities

---

3. NATCA, n.d.

of Atlanta, Chicago, Los Angeles, Dallas, and Denver. Many pilots live in and around these busy metropolitans.

For travel overseas, passengers can hopscotch from one airport to another until they can board an international flight. From international airports like Miami, pilots take travelers to South America and the Caribbean. From Los Angeles, pilots ferry passengers across the Pacific Ocean to Australia and Japan.

 ## Fast Fact

Most pilots who fly for 30 years will average between 15 and 20 million miles of flight during their lifetime. That's over 800 times around the earth for 20 million miles of flying. That's a lot of real estate!

Pilots in the United States fly to places all over the world, along with the rest of their lucky crew. They have opportunities to see new cultures, and sometimes, learn second and third languages. From New York, pilots can fly to England, France, Israel, or Turkey. Because it is also an international airport, New Yorkers can fly direct to places like Peru or Puerto Rico. It usually costs passengers more to fly internationally, but it also depends on the time of year. A commercial airline pilot, even when he or she is not working, gets to fly for free or a small service charge, even outside of the United States.

 ## From the cockpit

Many pilots say the best flights they've ever had include seeing the amazing sunsets from different parts of the world. Others say it was their first ever flight as a Captain. ∎

CHAPTER 5

Safety and Communication

Airspace is a word used to describe the room available in the sky for aircraft to move around in. Around the world, our airspace is becoming more and more crowded, despite the safe distance rules that keep aircraft separated. Rules have changed over the years so that more planes can occupy more sections of airspace, but many people feel that the decreased limits are dangerous. When you add in the introduction of today's drones, **collision avoidance** takes on a whole new meaning.

 **Fast Fact**

The FAA predicted at least 600,000 drones would be in the skies by the end of 2017.

The development of aircraft and scheduled air travel relied on aeronautical science and research. The **National Advisory Committee for Aeronautics** (NACA) was initially responsible for those tasks. In 1958, the agency closed, and its resources and people transferred to the newly-created National Aeronautics and Space Administration (NASA). NASA evolved into one of the world's leading aeronautical research centers. Its headquarters is located in Washington D.C., but it has facilities across the United States.

Additionally, creation of the **National Transportation Safety Board (NTSB)** helped to officially investigate accidents, determine probable cause, and make recommendations to avoid accident repetition. They have played a key role in improving air travel safety for all. Every time there is a commercial airline disaster, the NTSB takes charge.

 **Fast Fact**

The NTSB can investigate any transportation accident. The list includes railways, boats, and even some fatal vehicle crashes on highways.

It's true that airspace is crowded these days. Larger jets with more seats might mean a reduction in that congestion. It could also mean fewer pilot jobs. However, if you are dreaming about a career in the cockpit, don't worry yet. It will be many years before the crowded skies yield to monster planes like the **A-380**. The A-380 is the world's largest airliner. It can cost up to a half billion dollars to build, so there aren't many. It can carry up to 853 passengers.

From the cockpit

"When you first start flying, controllers are kind of intimidating, but after you fly more you realize that they are really there for you and to help keep everyone safe. Usually controllers are fun and great to talk to..." ■

Keeping planes separated today are **air traffic controllers (ATC)**. Air traffic controllers work for the Federal Aviation Administration (FAA). They guide planes from the gates, down painted lines on a taxiway that roll them across runways until they reach the number one position for take-off.

At the departure end of the runway planes line up like ducks in a row, and one by one are given permission to depart into the skies on a certain flight path that will keep them out of the way of other aircraft coming in to land on different runways. It's quite an orchestrated event.

From the cockpit

"You can never win an argument with an ATC, so don't bother unless you know you're right. In the end, recorded tapes can always be pulled and reviewed, but most of us would rather avoid that." ■

There are about 14,000 air traffic controllers nationwide.[4] They work from air traffic control towers on the airports controlling air traffic around the airport. They also work in buildings, called centers, spread out across the country. Once the aircraft leaves the airspace controlled by the airport, ATC hands the pilot off to the next controller along the route, whether that's at a center or a nearby tower if the plane isn't going far.

An air traffic controller is hired by the FAA after taking certain tests and evaluations. Many learn to control traffic in the military and cross over into the government job. Others "walk in" off the street with high school or college degrees. There are also universities that provide paths to the air traffic control career through aeronautical classes and student programs. Like pilots, one only needs to study and test well to be given an opportunity to enter a tower to see if they have the "right stuff."

4. FAA, 2017

From the cockpit

"Air traffic controllers are professionals, too, and conduct themselves as such. That being said, there are times when it can be difficult. Some talk so fast it's hard to understand them, some get short with you real quickly. At other times, they are guilty of the same misgivings they are terse with you about, such as not answering a radio call promptly. Overall though, it's a cooperative and easy relationship." ■

Once hired, the serious training begins. It can take years. Some controllers are trained at the official training location for ATC in Oklahoma City, Oklahoma. After passing through the channels of preparation, the air traffic controller is assigned to either an airport tower or a regional center.

General knowledge like airplane models, aviation laws, and the basics of flight are just the beginning for a controller at a new facility. The local airspace must be learned, along with other aviation facilities, including small and private airports. The controller must learn to speak the language, especially the hundreds if not thousands of abbreviations and acronyms used by pilots and other controllers.

From the cockpit

"Air traffic controllers, especially in the United States, are very professional and a pleasure to work with. In my 37 years of flying, I have nothing but good to say. Controllers in other countries are also very good. The biggest problem in other countries is their accent. Sometimes it's difficult to understand, but we always worked out the communications." ■

There is much to learn. Airports have many different abbreviated names for controllers, pilots, and other airline employees to use. Airports are given three-letter identifiers. For example, Atlanta-Hartsfield Airport is considered the busiest airport in the world. Pilots and controllers don't call it Atlanta-Hartsfield; they identify it as ATL. In other words, if you flew to Atlanta, you would find a tag on your baggage with the code ATL, the same acronym used by your pilot and air traffic control to identify your destination.

Here are some other airport identifiers. It is one of the first things memorized by new pilots and controllers, too!

Anchorage International
Airport = ANC

Dulles International Airport
(Washington D.C.) = IAD

Phoenix Sky Harbor International
Airport = PHX

Orlando International
Airport = MCO

Los Angeles International
Airport = LAX

Honolulu International
Airport = HNL

Denver International
Airport = DEN

O'Hare International Airport
(Chicago) = ORD

New York, John F Kennedy
International Airport = JFK

New Orleans International
Airport = MSY

Working together, pilots and air traffic controllers keep the skies friendly and safe. Without ATC on the radio, it would be difficult to navigate through the crowded skies and bad weather, not to mention their assistance in finding the best way to arrive or depart a maze of airport runways.

 ***Fast Fact***

As of 2017, Atlanta-Hartsfield Airport has five parallel runways. The controllers there work an average of 2,800 "operations" a day. An operation consists of an airplane landing or departing.

Weather

Weather has a major impact on comfort and safety of a flight. Even on clear, sunny days, pilots must be aware of activity in the atmosphere and what might be encountered along the way to their destination.

Weather that may affect flight includes fog, wind, snow, and thunderstorms. Fog reduces visibility, meaning it makes it hard to see. This is important on taxiways, and pulling in and out of gates. High winds are especially dangerous. They can interfere with taking off or landing the airplane. There is also a burst of wind called a **microburst**. Microbursts are columns or drafts of air that move downward fast and sharp. This can push an aircraft down into the ground.

Bad winter weather like snow and ice make it difficult to see as well. Worse, it can make taxiways and runways slippery. A plane cannot fly with frost or ice on its wings. You may have seen airport employees spraying planes down in the winter. They are "de-icing" the wings for safety.

 ### *Fast Fact*

On August 2nd, 1985, the crew of Delta Air Lines Flight 191 decided to fly through a thunderstorm. The airplane encountered a microburst of air on approach to the Dallas/Fort Worth airport. The microburst pushed the plane down, and it crashed just over a mile from the runway.

Yes, severe weather can literally overstress the airframe of a modern jetliner causing an in-flight breakup. The trick to preventing this is reading the weather and avoiding those severe conditions. That is the pilot's responsibility, along with weather reports and ATC.

Pilots receive weather reports from **meteorologists** and dispatchers, as well as air traffic controllers when necessary. Most major airlines have their own meteorology department to monitor and report weather. There are also **dispatchers**. Dispatchers, much like air traffic control, monitor an airline company's flight from start to finish. They are available to the pilots if there is a problem, and can also warn the cockpit of any bad weather or other emergencies they need to know.

It's important to remember that almost all experiences flying in bad weather are just that — experiences. Nothing can replace the experience gained by working through and around severe weather elements in the cockpit. It's important to learn how to dodge bad weather. If a captain has hundreds of hours flying through rain, sleet, snow, ice, and around thunderstorms and tornadoes, he or she will usually be much better poor-weather pilots than those with limited exposure.

From the cockpit

"A good day is good weather." ■

The basic criteria for holding the Airline Transport Certificate (ATP) that allows you to fly as pilot-in-command is the same for captains flying 50-passenger planes as it is for a Boeing 777 captain flying 450 people. All pilots are trained for bad weather. An in-depth FAA written test that covers advanced weather knowledge and a many other aviation subjects, plus an exhausting airplane check-ride must be passed before being issued the ATP certificate.

Fast Fact

Pilots pursuing an ATP certificate must have logged a minimum of 1,500 hours and must complete an ATP certification training program that includes weather training. The program consists of 30 hours of ground school plus 10 hours of simulator training prior to being eligible to take the ATP written and practical tests. The 10 hours of simulator training includes six hours of training in a full-motion simulator.

Why is all of the training so important? A flight instructor teaching private pilots to fly light single engine airplanes can easily accumulate 1,500 hours flight time in a year and a half with very little exposure to bad weather. Without the additional training requirement, That person could legally be at the controls of your airliner during a winter storm.

Some pilots feel the one thing the ATP certificate fails to demand is the *type* of flying or equipment used in acquiring the first 1,500 hours of your flight time. Anyone could have heavy transport time from the military or time only in a light airplane like our flight instructor example.

What does this have to do with bad weather captains? Everything!

Experience in this occupation is what separates the amateurs from the pros. Flying jetliners in bad weather is not automatically assigned to the most skilled pilots. Airline crews bid schedules based on seniority and days off, so weather flying is not a part of the trip selection process. Weather forecasting is still somewhat of an imperfect science.

 ### *From the cockpit*

"On one occasion we encountered severe turbulence [rough air] to the point where maintaining altitude and aircraft control became difficult. We notified ATC of our situation and were informed there were no other aircraft in the area, so we could vary our altitude as needed. We divided up duties in the cockpit and maintained our altitude and speed as best we could. It only lasted about five minutes, but it was an intense five minutes." ■

Older pilots, unless they started late in life with a career change, are less likely to make judgment errors when flying into rough weather. Also, small, regional airlines are more conscious about crew pairings than they have been in the past. Matching skill levels (inexperienced pilots flying with more experienced aviators) is an ongoing task for airline companies and government lawmakers.

The current FAA regulations require the Pilot-In-Command to make all takeoffs and landings in certain situations if the second-in-command, or co-pilot, has fewer than 100 hours of flight time in that type aircraft. Regulations also prohibit operations unless either pilot has at least 75 hours of flight time in the type of airplane being flown.

What does this mean to you? For starters it resolves some issues regarding experience levels in the cockpit. All pilots start out with zero experience, especially where weather flying is concerned. New pilots entering the airline ranks are watched carefully as they develop, and airlines and the FAA are doing all they can to assure that your crew is up to the job.

From the cockpit

"Good training and experience win the day." ∎

All major U.S. airlines have superb dispatch and meteorology departments that can contact a plane in flight. These folks are the shepherds tending the weather. With their assistance, flights can usually be given smoother route alternatives. In addition, pilots frequently give "ride reports" that assist others in selecting route and altitudes for a smoother ride. These so-called "ride reports" are often the best sort of in-flight weather information.

Sometimes, despite our best efforts, it's impossible to find smooth air. Pilots often joke among themselves. They label those unavoidable bumpy rides as "passenger appreciation flights."

From the cockpit

"Honestly, we don't like bumps either — it spills our coffee." ∎

Here's the rub about weather avoidance: sometimes captains misjudgment or wait too long before asking for help from dispatch or air traffic control. Regrettably, they can become trapped in a weather system with no smooth way out.

As a pilot, written tests or check rides will partially evaluate your weather knowledge. However, it's important for even experienced pilots to remember that Mother Nature is unpredictable and doesn't play by any rules.

Mechanics and Operations

The likelihood of an average person being involved in an airliner accident is similar to the odds of being struck by lightning. Flying in a modern jet liner captained by an experience pilot is statistically the safest mode of transportation in the world — even more so than walking.

There are some statistics that say half of all aviation accidents are "pilot error" meaning a mistake was made by the pilot, but there are other reasons for aviation disasters. It's easy to blame a pilot when an accident happens, but experts admit that it isn't quite fair. Often, a pilot does not survive, and the real cause is related to several different things that went wrong at the same time.

 ***Fast Fact***

On January 15, 2009, US Airways Flight 1549 departed from LaGuardia Airport in New York. The Airbus A320-214 left the runway, and shortly after takeoff suffered bird strikes in both engines. Thrust was lost in both engines, but the crew was able to land the plane into the Hudson River without crashing. All 107 people aboard survived.

Despite the billions of dollars spent on aircraft design and the training of crews to fly them, occasional accidents do happen. Some are survivable, while others are not. Most fatal accidents start with a small problem that rapidly becomes a major problem. If managed properly in the early stages, the odds of survival increase.

Some experts insist mechanical problems are the second cause of airline disasters while others list if further down. No matter how often they are to blame, bad maintenance or inspections, a flaw in the airplane's design, or a mistake made when the craft was manufactured at the factory can cause these problems.

 ***Fast Fact***

The Aviation Safety Network reports that there were 163 aviation accidents around the world in 2016. Of these accidents, there were only 24 fatalities.[5] This means your chance of not surviving an airplane crash, even if one were to happen, is very small. In fact, it's more dangerous to drive a car down the highway!

According to the scientific aviation article *Why Aircraft Fail*, some common aircraft mechanical failures include **corrosion**, **fatigue**, **brittle fractures**, overloading, and wear and tear from **abrasion** (rubbing) and **erosion**.[6]

If this sounds like a mouthful, it's important to understand that corrosion is the breaking down or wearing away of metal. This can happen naturally in an outdoor environment. Have you ever left a bicycle outside and later found the chain to be rusty? When metal becomes weak, it can't support the weight or other stresses that affect its job. In other words, when metal parts of the airplane wear out, they need to be replaced. That's why airplane mechanics must inspect the plane on a regular basis.

Fatigue in engineering means cracking. Cracks can occur when parts are exposed to unexpected forces, or just from the same action happening over and over. Have you ever dropped an egg? The egg can only handle so much force; if it's treated too roughly, there's going to be a messy disaster! The principle of brittle fracturing is similar to fatigue. In brittle fractures, a heavy load is added too quickly and parts snap.

5. Aviation Safety, n.d.
6. Findlay, Harrison, 2002

From the cockpit

"I can't think of any occupation other than astronaut or test pilot that provides such a work environment." ∎

Aircraft maintenance is very expensive. However, most everyday mechanical problems like a burned-out light bulb are not that hard to repair. In fact, it's normal to have mechanics checking or making small repairs while a plane is at the gate. This might mean a later departure time, and that passengers might have to wait, but it is always better to be safe than sorry. Airlines and pilots understand that. Of course, it's important for paying passengers to understand that, too!

More serious issues that must be maintained or replaced for safety include contaminated air or heating systems, contaminated fuel systems, water drainage systems, worn engine blades, and even the engines themselves.

An aircraft, whether private or commercial, will always need maintenance. At an airline, it is normal for a licensed airplane mechanic to run down a checklist after every single flight before an airplane can leave on its next flight. There may also be other checks every three days, weekly, and monthly. You can expect to see a commercial craft towed to a hanger for service after several hundred hours of flight. This keeps everything in working order.

 **_Fast Fact_**

About 95 percent of passengers have survived aircraft disasters since 1983.[7]

It is easy to imagine that when a system fails in the cockpit, a pilot can become distracted or concerned. Flying a jet seven to eight times faster than people drive on the freeway as well as being miles above the earth is a great deal of pressure. That's approximately 550 miles per hour! Problem solving becomes a matter of life and death. Sometimes issues need to be solved in seconds. A pilot cannot just pull over, hit pause, or have a mechanic take a look at the problem later. Everything is important, and mistakes can be deadly.

Fortunately, more often than not, when things do go wrong, pilots are so well prepared for such instances they are able to land the plane safely.

---

7. Aviation Safety, n.d.

 ### *Fast Fact*

The worst plane crash blamed on mechanical problems happened in 1985 when a Japan Airline Boeing 747 flew into a mountainside and killed over 500 people. A rear pressure bulkhead, a part found in the tail of aircraft, burst apart. This led to a loss of control from the cockpit, which meant tragedy for everyone on board.

New pilots and passengers should take comfort that in every rare aviation accident that occurs, there is always an investigation to determine the cause of the failure. The data collected from accident investigations are used to improve training, mechanical and computer systems, and even the aircraft themselves.

 ### *From the cockpit*

"Our airplanes record everything we do, and the airlines review all of the data all of the time. It is like driving your car, and then the police review your driving data and give you a ticket if you sped or did anything wrong. There is a lot more regulatory stress in today's flying than in the old days. Even in the military, the pilots turn on the cameras before they go into battle and get second guessed on every detail." ∎

Technology is still advancing and aviation continues to improve. This mean mechanics and operations for airplanes are getting better, too. When things do happen, it's important to remember that lessons will be learned.

Unidentified Flying Objects (UFOs)

People often wonder if there are dangers in the clouds that come from out of this world. With all of the stories and legends about strange lights or spaceships in the skies, it's no wonder a new pilot might be curious about what's up in the atmosphere besides airplanes.

From the cockpit

"Have I ever seen a UFO? Nope!" ■

An unknown object in the sky is called an **Unidentified Flying Object** or UFO. Many manmade things are often mistaken for something mysterious. Besides airplanes, the earth's atmosphere has weather balloons, telescopes, satellites, tools, plastics, and even flecks of paint. We also have the International Space Station orbiting the planet.

Fast Fact

According to National Geographic, there are more than 8,000 objects floating in the skies surrounding the earth.[8]

All of this "space junk" can reflect light at just the right time and can appear to be another type of aircraft.

---

8. National Geographic, n.d.

The first recorded UFO sighting in America was actually a long time ago. In 1639, John Winthrop was the governor of the Massachusetts Bay Colony. Along with other religious English Puritans, he had come to a strange land for freedom and a new life. In his historic diary, he wrote about something strange that happened to an honorable man named James Everall.

Mr. Everall and two other men were in a boat on the Muddy River. It was night, and in the sky they suddenly saw a light that stood still then "flamed up." The men swore the light changed into the shape of a "swine" and then ran back and forth across the sky "as swift as an arrow" for several hours. The governor wrote that other respectable people around Charlestown also saw the same mysterious event.

From the cockpit

"On several occasions I have seen things I could not explain. I talked to ATC each time, and they had nothing on their radar in any of the cases. In one case, it moved so fast it was impossible for it to be another aircraft. I still don't know what it was that we saw." ∎

That wasn't the only UFO sighting for the pilgrim. Along with others, Governor Winthrop recorded a few other sightings of strange lights and even visitors made of light. All of the witnesses were respectable members of the community and more than one person witnessed the events. At the time, the pilgrims believed they were witnessing strange events of ghosts and devils.

From the cockpit

"I've been a licensed pilot for almost 50 years. Of the 196 countries on earth, I have flown over all of them but 16 and landed in most. During that time, I only remember two occasions at night where I observed, along with the other pilot, lights in the sky that had a nonlinear, random-like motion. On both occasions, we contacted air traffic control and asked if they had radar contact with the traffic we were observing high above us. We thought it might be extremely high altitude secret military operations. One encounter was a single target, the other about a half dozen objects that were in a loose formation. Neither encounter was picked up by ATC. Were they UFOs, secret military tests, or just aberrations? I honestly don't know. On both occasions the other pilot and I watched these unidentifiable objects for several minutes. So, I guess my truthful answer would have to be, yes I've seen flying objects that I couldn't identify. I have not seen little green men, been abducted or followed by any Men In Black after these events. This was just a late night observation of extremely fast, randomly-moving, bright objects in front of my plane. That's the whole truth and nothing but the truth." ■

The first recognized modern sighting of an UFO is considered to be from Mr. Kenneth Arnold in 1947. Arnold was flying his own private small plane near Mount Rainer in the state of Washington, when he spotted nine objects.

According to Arnold, the objects were shaped like crescents and moved very fast like they were skipping across water. His report created the word "flying saucer" we use today, because the newspaper confused his description, saying the objects were saucer-shaped instead of formed like crescents. Since that time, there have been hundreds of thousands of "flying saucer" sightings reported across the country.

 ***Fast Fact***

Mount Rainer is actually a volcano and the highest mountain in the state of Washington. It is considered one of the most prominent peaks in the United States.

Because of so many strange sightings in the skies, the U.S. Air Force started an organization in 1948 to investigate them, called "Project Sign." The investigators soon decided that most of the UFO reports were aircraft from the Soviet Union. Only a few would wonder out loud if there were ships from outer space visiting.

The same events happened around the world, so not everyone was convinced of the easy answer. However, secret tests of military equipment in the Soviet Union were known to create UFO reports in that country, and the Soviet government encouraged the idea of UFOs to hide what they were really working on. It made sense to scientists that the same things were happening everywhere else, and it is a common explanation for the events today.

From the cockpit

"I was flying very early in the morning over New York City, and we saw a really bright, shining object high in the sky, and it was moving fast. The sun was coming up on the horizon, so it was light, and this object was really fast. It took us about five minutes before we realized it was the International Space Station reflecting off the sun. It was really cool." ■

So are UFOs still reported today? The answer to that is "yes." However, with advanced science and technology, we understand that our eyes and minds can play tricks on us. For example, fast-moving aircraft can be seen "speeding" across the sky. Sometimes stationary objects like a bright planet can appear to follow us, when it is we, who are in fact, moving. There are also optical illusions created by reflections in cameras, glasses, and windows that trick our brains.

For those who point to radar evidence of UFOs, it's important to remember that some natural or manmade things show up on radar besides aircraft. Weather, gases, and events from space like meteors can also affect equipment.

From the cockpit

"All of us have seen something we couldn't posi-
tively identify. It's especially difficult to identify
things at night when you just see some lights go by.
I did see a huge weather balloon that was over
60,000 feet up, and that was interesting. Some real fast military planes
have zipped by. That's it. Really, I think there is too much media hype
about UFOs." ■

With all of the thousands of flights across the world every day, it's safe to
say pilots have a bird's eye view to anything mysterious. With so few reports from actual cockpit crews to prove anything is "out there," you can
rest assured you are in no danger from unidentified flying objects.

Cockpit Communications

So what else can create safety problems besides weather and mechanical
failures? Sometimes the problem is not created by a mechanical glitch at all,
but by poor or confusing communication.

 ***Fast Fact***

Communication is so important in the workplace today, it's a college degree!

The technical phrase used for communication between people is **Interpersonal Communication**. This is such an important skill, it is taught in college. Interpersonal communication is when people exchange words or feelings with words (verbal), body language (non-verbal), or behaviors, to send messages and interpret them.

When we don't understand one another clearly or consider something from a different perspective, it can create conflict. Throughout a pilot's career, he or she will deal with different types and levels of conflict on a daily basis. Decisions will be required, and sometimes not everyone will agree.

 ***From the cockpit***

"I can't think of an office with more potential for conflict than a modern airline cockpit. Here's why: Lock yourself in a closet-size office with someone who's normally opinionated (as most pilots are), and eventually, despite your best efforts to get along or agree, it just doesn't happen. It's human nature. We don't always like or agree with the decisions of others — especially when they might put your life in jeopardy. Fortunately, most flight deck crews work hard at avoiding this showdown of opinions." ■

It still remains a respected practice for the captain to have the final say on the operation of the aircraft. However, because of accidents in the past, things have changed. Today, there's a distinct difference in the way decisions are now made in the airline cockpit.

Crew Resource Management

Crew resource management (CRM) is a term you will need to know. It's also known by other names, such as cockpit resource management or flight-deck resource management. It was a term coined by a NASA psychologist named John Lauber. For several years, Lauber studied the communication that was happening in aircraft cockpits. The idea that the captain in the left seat was a god was observed to be alive and well. However, one thing became obvious to Lauber. Better communication between crewmembers actually made the cockpit safer. Goodbye god — hello team player.

CRM finally came about after experts examined the 1978 crash of United Airlines Flight 173. In this accident, the crew ran the plane out of gas while trying to solve a landing gear problem. After the crash investigation, the NTSB made a revolutionary recommendation to require CRM training for all airline crews. There are many pilots who feel this is one of the best recommendations to ever come from a government agency.

In the history of aviation, communication in the cockpit or to outside resources was never encouraged since most airlines were only concerned about their pilots keeping on schedule and not breaking the equipment. That giant job was dumped squarely on the captain's shoulders. It's easy to understand why some crewmembers might have thought of stressed captains as jerks. They had to be, considering the environment they operated in and all of things that were their responsibility.

From the cockpit

"I've never met an airline captain who didn't have an entertaining story about a mistake he'd made. Most were silly forgetful things, while other events were more serious, but ended on a high note. Regardless, the cockpit of an airliner is where mistakes should be as few as humanly possible." ■

With CRM, Lauber proposed making the cockpit culture less strict. Co-pilots and flight engineers were suddenly encouraged to question captains if they observed them making mistakes. This was not easily accepted by some of the older captains, but they would eventually come to accept the new concept, although reluctantly.

In 1981, United Airline was the first to provide CRM training for cockpit crews. They had no desire for a repeat of Flight 173. By the 1990s, CRM training for aircrews had gone global. With the acceptance of CRM concepts, the captain's role in the cockpit has been re-defined. Yes, the captain still has the final say, but his decisions are now more informed.

 ***Fast Fact***

If you want to see a good example of the need for CRM, take a look at the 1954 classic John Wayne movie ***The High and the Mighty***. John Wayne portrays a very vocal, washed-up co-pilot that ends up saving the day on a trans-Pacific flight.

One of the first problems CRM education faced was defining how cockpit communication could be more effective. At first, some vocal first officers and engineers thought they now had equal say in the command of the aircraft. Sadly, this brought about more than one heated conversation in the cockpit. Needless to say, the early change caused a few problems.

The purpose of CRM was to allow all crewmembers freedom to speak their minds and challenge what they interpreted as a bad call by the captain. As one can imagine, this didn't always come about as intended. It took a while before everyone got on board and understood that in order for cockpit communication to be effective, all parties including the captain must handle the new philosophy carefully.

CRM concepts have spread out of the cockpit and into other totally different work cultures.

From the cockpit

"A close doctor friend of mine invited me to observe a complicated surgical procedure and to see how he worked. This was over 20 years ago. He was terrific to watch, but the assisting surgeon was demanding, abusive, and clearly viewed with contempt by the scrub nurses and everyone else in the operating room. After the surgery, 'Wow' was all I could say to my friend. Talk about different types of surgeons! I asked my friend if hospitals or even medical schools provided training like CRM. He had no idea what I was talking about. Since then, many hospitals have initiated resource management for surgeons and operating room staff. That call was greatly needed." ■

Captains have become more effective today with the adoption of CRM principles. For older pilots who have been around, it's a relief to know that the airlines are now fully on board with CRM. They remind captains, and other crewmembers, at every opportunity of all the resources available to aid them in the decision-making process. Two or three brains working together in the cockpit are far better than one. Now, factor in the entire airline and FAA resources that can assist a pilot, and a cockpit and crew have powerful problem-solving tools.

From the cockpit

"For those inclined to think that the captain is the only one flying the plane and making all the occasional death-stopping decisions — think again.

There's still only one captain, but he or she now takes advantage of many different brains.

Being the person in charge of an airliner's safety can be the loneliest position on earth." ■

What does all this mean for you? You may be too young to be married right now, but interaction between a captain and crew is described as being best when everyone treats it like a happy marriage.

Captains are paid to be calm, orderly problem solvers. While not all of them can do that all of the time, they certainly try. For someone to "have a chip on his shoulder" in the cockpit is rare, but it does happen. The hard truth is some people in this world just have difficulty in getting along.

Professionally speaking, most pilots that fly for commercial airlines are not only intelligent, they are wise enough to notice personality problems early on. If a pilot sees a potential conflict with another personality, he or she will usually say something. This is important, because bad feelings can cause poor communication and jeopardize a safe operating environment.

Remember, all pilots have licenses that can be revoked, or taken away, by the FAA. The possibility of losing this hard-to-get job is a good reason to behave. If a clash starts while sitting at the gate, the quick simple cure is to leave the cockpit and get a replacement crew. However, this usually means an unpleasant trip to the Chief Pilot's office for both people.

 ## Did you know?

The practice of good CRM skills isn't just for captains.

A good crew can count on each other when things get busy.

Confrontations are for hostile individuals.

Sincere discussions are reserved for concerned professionals.

In the cockpit, the pro listens and the fool argues.

If you know you're right, convince the other pilot. All pilots are logical thinkers.

The other pilot can save your life, so why not work together.

Being right is not always the correct answer to a confrontation. Because of this, pilots seem to have a better grasp of how to deal with confrontations. Maybe it's because of the "locked-in-a-box" occupation. Regardless, a conflict can be dangerous in the cockpit. If you want to be a captain and your life is perpetually filled with conflict, you might consider keeping your occupation choices on the ground.

 ## From the cockpit

"Conflicts in the cockpit can and do happen. Keeping your character in check is a sign of maturity. Taking the easy and safe way out of a confrontation takes courage and compassion. Arm yourself with both." ■

When Things Go Wrong

The airline captain isn't just responsible for safety and communication in the cockpit; he or she is solely responsible for the overall safety of a flight. What exactly does this statement mean when things go terribly wrong?

Captain Lindsay Fenwick of Northwest Airlines, and Michael Huhn, ALPA Senior Staff Engineer, wrote the following:

> *"An accident, by definition, is an occurrence that is not expected, foreseen, or intended. By this definition, then, an accident is not a crime. In English Common Law, a crime requires two elements — intending to commit an unlawful act and actually committing the deed. Most airline accidents are just that — unfortunate and unforeseen consequences of human error, not necessarily the pilots'."*[9]

Punishment for a pilot or crewmember, real or threatened, can have a bad effect on the behavior of the person being questioned in an accident investigation. This affects the quality of the investigation, too, which makes it harder to find the truth. So, why do most stories seem to spotlight pilots as the bad guys? It's usually misinformation or media hype.

Of course, the easiest answer is because pilots are at the "pointy" end of the plane, and are usually the first to feel the impact of a crash. The captain is always the individual with ultimate **accountability**. That's why he is boss in the cockpit.

---

9. Fenwick, Huhn. 2003

From the cockpit

"Pilots are the good guys; it's the system of unjustified blame that vilifies us and slows the healing process after an air disaster. Yes, we'll gladly take the blame if it means saving lives in the future, so that's why the buck stops with us!" ∎

Let's take a look at what commonly happens after a crash: first, the surviving flight crews are advised to provide written statements and interviews to the National Transportation Safety Board (NTSB) and other organizations. Next, this information will become public record and eventually obtained by both the employer and the FAA. The media will be waiting, too. Then there are the unavoidable consequences.

The costs of being involved in a commercial airline accident can include company discipline like required additional training, unpaid time off, or being fired. There may also be suspension or fines. In fact, the problems after an accident can be as stressful for a pilot as the accident itself!

However, rest assured, pilots are protected by laws and unions when they do their duty. In the United States, when a pilot acts in what he or she perceives to be in the best interest of safe aircraft operation, the understanding is that they will not be criminally prosecuted. Based on this assurance, and in spite of the possible unhappy outcome of telling the whole truth and nothing but the truth, pilots are encouraged to fully cooperate and do everything they can to help in accident investigations.

From the cockpit

"Many accidents are a result of operational or mechanical issues that can't be resolved in the air. Accident investigation has played a vital role in identifying mechanical, operational, and human factors issues that need to be addressed. This investigative process, and

the resulting knowledge gained from sad, catastrophic accidents, en-
ables us to prevent them from happening again. This is what an airline
accident investigation should be about; not placing blame on the
crew." ∎

Unfortunately, deceased pilots make great targets for lawyers seeking
wrongful death compensation (money) for victims. This can be very unfair.
Almost all of the time, the public can count on the fact that captains on
commercial airlines are experienced and extremely cautious. Yes, they make
mistakes, but in normal situations never on purpose. Sadly, that does not
stop attorneys from trying to prosecute them.

As stated before, airline accidents are very rare. With over 87,000 flights in
the United States every day[10], it's a comfort to know there are professional,
trained pilots navigating us through the friendly skies.

---

10. NATCA, n.d.

Infamous Aviation Events

The Wright Brothers' Deadly Flight

Orville and Wilbur Wright do not only receive credit for flying the first powered airplane, they were also involved in the first passenger death to ever occur in an airplane. It happened only five years after the first powered flight, and the victim's name was Lieutenant Thomas Selfridge.

The Wright brothers did not stop with the invention of a flying machine in 1903. The next two years after their success in North Carolina, they continued improving the powered airplane. In addition, they tried to figure out a way to turn the idea of flight into a solid, successful business.

 *Fast Fact*

The Wright Brothers were published in many magazines. In *Century* Magazine they wrote about their childhood:

"Late in the autumn of 1878, our father came into the house one evening with some object partly concealed in his hands, and before we could see what it was, he tossed it into the air. Instead of falling to the floor, as we expected, it flew across the room till it struck the ceiling, where it fluttered awhile, and finally sank to the floor. It was a little toy, known to scientists as a "hélicoptère," but which we, with sublime disregard for science, at once dubbed a "bat." It was a light frame of cork and bamboo, covered with paper, which formed two screws, driven in opposite directions by rubber bands under torsion. A toy so delicate lasted only a short time in the hands of small boys, but its memory was abiding."[11]

The United States government was not interested in any of the Wrights' ideas at first. Refusing to give up, the brothers went overseas and caught the attention of officials in England and France. Finally, in 1907, a French business offered them a contract. Then the U.S. Army decided to get on board, too.

For the Army, the brothers were challenged with building an airplane that could hold two men and fly faster than 40 miles per hour.

 **_Fast Fact_**

The Army contract with the Wright Brothers promised them $25,000 if they were successful.

Wilbur Wright went to France to make more sales. Orville Wright got to work in Kitty Hawk, North Carolina, with two mechanics: Charlie Taylor and Charlie Furnas. They did several test flights and set records.

Once the airplane built for the Army was ready, Orville Wright sent it to Fort Myer, Virginia, along with his helpers. The invention was sent in a crate and stored in a balloon hanger until Orville could join the others.

---

11. Wright, 1908

The time finally came to prep the aircraft and show it off. However, the inventors had some problems to figure out. It wouldn't reach 40 miles an hour, and that meant losing money on the deal. They solved the problem with higher **octane** gas and new **oil cups**. The trick worked, and Orville flew it over Fort Myer for the first time on September 3, 1908. Within a week, he could fly for about an hour and take a passenger with him.

The success of the Wright brothers' newest airplane and whether not the Army would pay them was to be decided by a committee of five officers, and one of them was Lieutenant Thomas Selfridge.

Selfridge was a member of the **Aerial Experiment Association**. He had designed and flown an airplane, too. Orville Wright did not like him right away. He felt like Selfridge was a competition and couldn't be trusted with information. He wrote to his brother, "He plans to meet me often at diner where he can pump me."[12]

On September 17, 1908, Orville was scheduled to take Lieutenant Selfridge up in the aircraft. He'd already flown over 15 times and set records up to 74 minutes long. The flight with Selfridge would be different. Unfortunately, at around three to four minutes in the air, things went wrong and went wrong fast.

Orville Wright flew over the parade grounds and made several circles then unexpectedly, he heard two loud thumping noises. The airplane became uncontrollable. It pitched nose down and dove straight into the earth.

---

12. Wright Brothers, n.d.

 **_Fast Fact_**

Orville Wright investigated his own accident and determined it was caused by a wooden propeller that split apart. A piece of the propeller hit a wire and caused damage to the aircraft's tail. Other "experts" agreed.

Charlie Taylor and Charlie Furnas reached the wrecked Wright plane first. Orville Wright was unconscious and bleeding. At the hospital, it was discovered he had a broken leg and broken ribs.

Lieutenant Selfridge was not so lucky. He was trapped in the wreck, and it took longer to get him out. At the hospital, doctors found he had a fractured skull and needed surgery. During the operation, Selfridge died. His death made him the first passenger to die in aviation's powered aircraft.

 *Fast Fact*

After the death of Lieutenant Thomas Selfridge, the Army required its pilots to wear helmets.

Despite the tragedy, the Army decided to continue with the Wright brothers' contract. Although Orville had not accomplished everything he had promised to do, the committee felt the model of the Wright Flyer would be a success. These first brothers of aviation started a company and sold airplanes to the United States and France, making them one of the first and most successful aviation companies of their time.

Tragedy in the Skies: 9/11

Were you born before September 11, 2001? Today we know it as **9/11**. It is the biggest aviation disaster in United States history.

 ## *Did you know?*

On September 11, 2001, terrorists hijacked, or took control of, four American airplanes. Two planes crashed into two skyscrapers in New York's World Trade Center. Another airplane was purposely crashed into the Pentagon. The final airplane crashed down in a field in the state of Pennsylvania before it could hit its target. Over 2,900 people lost their lives in a matter of minutes. Many died as heroes.

What happened in the aftermath of the 9/11 tragedies was devastating for every United States citizen, but airlines in particular were affected, especially from an economic standpoint. Many people decided flying would no longer be safe. Airline ticket sales fell to almost nothing; more importantly, the trust people once had that airlines could keep passengers safe was destroyed.

Almost immediately following the attack, all aircraft flying over the United States or even just approaching the country were ordered to land. The automatic confusion was an expensive nightmare for the airlines and an unimaginable inconvenience for passengers scattered across the landscape. The rental car companies made a fortune, but some airlines had to use almost all of their financial credit up to dangerous levels just to keep the doors open.

 ## *From the cockpit*

"On the early morning of September 11, 2001, I was in Minneapolis, Minnesota, at my airlines training center getting a check ride in a Boeing 757-200 simulator. It was still dark when I entered the simulator at 6:00 a.m. At the halfway point of the ride, we took a break to stretch our legs. In the reception area of the training center, a small crowd had gathered around a portable TV and everyone watched as looped footage played over and over, showing an American Airlines Boeing 767 crash into the North tower of the World Trade Center.

"No one spoke — all eyes stared at the tiny TV screen as the drama unfolded.

Eighteen minutes later, a United Airlines Boeing 767 crashed into the south tower near its 60th floor. I don't know if it's possible, but I swear not one of us breathed during those 18 minutes." ■

For those too young to know or who have forgotten, the following script is a timeline of events surrounding the 9/11 attacks. The planes involved that tragic day were American Airlines Flight 11, American Airlines Flight 77, United Flight 175, and United Flight 93.

9/11 Timeline of events

— **8:00 a.m.:** American Airlines Flight 11, carrying 81 passengers and 11 crew-members, begins its takeoff from Logan Airport in Boston, Massachusetts en route to Los Angeles.

— **8:13 a.m.:** An air traffic controller instructs American 11 to climb to 35,000 feet, and the aircraft fails to respond. The controller tries using the emergency frequency to contact the aircraft, but there is no response.

— **8:14 a.m.:** United Airlines Flight 175, carrying 56 passengers and nine crew-members on board, takes off from Logan Airport in Boston, Massachusetts.

— **8:20 a.m.:** American Flight 77 takes off from Dulles International Airport.

— **8:21 a.m.:** American Flight 11 turns off its **transponder**.

— **8:24 a.m.:** A transmission from a hijacker comes from American 11:

"We have some planes. Just stay quiet, and you'll be okay. We are returning to the airport" ("We have some planes," was unintelligible.) Seconds later another statement follows: "Nobody move. Everything will be okay. If you try to make any moves, you'll endanger yourself and the airplane. Just stay quiet."

— **8:28 a.m.:** Boston Center calls the FAA Command Center in Herndon, Virginia, and reports that American 11 has been **hijacked**.

— **8:34 a.m.:** Boston Center receives another transmission from American 11: "Nobody move, please. We are going back to the airport. Don't try to make any stupid moves."

— **8:37 a.m.:** Boston Center informs NORAD of American 11's hijacking. It is the first notice the military receives of the unfolding events.

FAA: "Hi. Boston Center TMU, we have a problem here. We have a hijacked aircraft headed towards New York, and we need you guys, we need someone to scramble some F-16s or something up there, help us out."

NORAD: "Is this real-world or exercise?"

FAA: "No, this is not an exercise, not a test."**8:41 a.m.:** United 175 enters New York airspace.

8:42 a.m.: United Flight 93 takes off from the airport in Newark, New Jersey.

8:46 a.m.: In response to American 11's hijacking, Otis Air Force Base receives an order to scramble F-15s. Military officials ask for a destination for the fighter planes, but no one knows. At the same time of the order, American 11 crashes into the World Trade Center's North Tower.

8:47 a.m.: United 175 changes its transponder code twice. The changes go unnoticed because the same controller assigned to it is looking for American 11.

8:48 a.m.: New York Center, unaware of American 11 crashing, talks to the FAA Command Center in a teleconference concerning that flight:

"This is New York Center. We're watching the airplane... They've told us that they believe one of their stewardesses was stabbed and that there are people in the cockpit that have control of the aircraft..."

8:50 a.m.: The military receives word that a plane has hit the World Trade Center. At the same time, American 77 ceases communication with air traffic controllers.

8:51 a.m.: An air traffic controller notices a change in the transponder code from United 175. The plane does not respond to repeat requests to change it back.

— **8:53 a.m.:** Military fighter jets summoned for American 11 are airborne, but still lack a target and information about the threat. At the same time, the air traffic controller tells a peer there is a second hijacking and United 175 is unaccounted for. The controller begins diverting planes from the path of United 175.

— **8:54 a.m.:** Indianapolis air traffic controllers notice American 77 deviating from its flight plan. The flight does not respond to contact, and controllers are unaware of the hijacking and crash in New York.

— **8:56 a.m.:** American 77 turns off its transponder.

— **9:00 a.m.:** Indianapolis Center notifies agencies that American 77 is missing, possibly crashed and seeks military help for a search and rescue.

— **9:01 a.m.:** New York Center notifies its command of its dilemma:

> "We have several situations going on here. It's escalating big, big time. We need to get the military involved with us."

— **9:02 a.m.:** New York Center asks New York's terminal approach control for help in finding United 175:

> **Terminal:** "I got somebody who keeps coasting, but it looks like he's going into one of the small airports down there. Got him just out of 9,500 — 9,000 now."
>
> **Boston Center:** "Do you know who he is?"
>
> **Terminal:** "...We don't know who he is. We're just picking him up now."
>
> **Boston Center:** "Heads up man, it looks like another one coming in."

— **9:03 a.m.:** United Airlines Flight 175 crashes into the South Tower of the World Trade Center. Boston Center deciphers the message from American 11, and realizes hijackers control more than one plane.

— **9:08 a.m. to 9:13 a.m.:** Military fighters hold a pattern over Long Island's coast. **NORAD** decides to ask the FAA to enter New York airspace as a defensive move.

> "... If this stuff is gonna keep on going, we need to take those fighters, put 'em over Manhattan. That's the best play right now."

9:10 a.m.: American 77 enters Washington Center airspace but goes undetected for 36 minutes as the FAA checks westerly points for the craft.

9:09 a.m.: Fighter jets in Langley, Virginia, move to battle stations to backup New York fighters who may get low on fuel.

9:17 a.m.: The Federal Aviation Administration shuts down all New York City area airports.

9:20 a.m.: Indianapolis Center learns about the other hijackings and becomes suspicious about American 77.

9:21 a.m.: The Port Authority of New York and New Jersey orders all bridges and tunnels in the New York area closed, and FAA Command Center tells Dulles terminal approach control to look for targets.

9:25 a.m.: The military establishes a combat air patrol over Manhattan, and the FAA issues a nation-wide ground stop of all aircraft.

9:28 a.m.: The FAA receives its last normal communication from United 93.

9:29 a.m.: Cleveland Center hears screams and struggles from an unknown source and someone yelling, "Get out of here! Get out of here!" The control center notices United 93 has dropped 700 feet.

9:30 a.m.: President George W. Bush, speaking in Sarasota, Florida, says the country has suffered an "apparent terrorist attack." Cleveland Center polls other flights to determine if they heard the screaming at 9:29. Several report they did.

9:32 a.m.: Dulles terminal approach control spots a suspicious aircraft and notifies the Secret Service. An unarmed National Guard cargo plane begins following American 77. Cleveland Center receives another transmission on the frequency from where there was screaming:

> "Keep remaining sitting. We have a bomb on board."

> (The transmitter selector panel, located on the center pedestal of the Boeing 757/767 is a maze of pushbuttons, switches, and glowing indicator lights. This and other inadvertent transmissions by the terrorist were likely caused by incorrect use of the selector panel.)

— **9:34 a.m.:** The FAA is notified that United 93 might have a bomb on board. Until 10:08, Cleveland Center provides the FAA updates on United 93's course.

— **9:36 a.m.:** NORAD learns of a suspicious aircraft a few miles from the White House and orders the Langley fighter jets back to Washington. Cleveland Center asks whether anyone has requested military interception of United 93.

— **9:38 a.m.:** American 77, with 58 passengers, four flight attendants and two pilots, crashes into the Pentagon. The National Guard pilot reports the crash to Washington's terminal facility. The Langley fighter jets are 150 miles away.

— **9:39 a.m.:** A radio transmission from United 93 is heard. It is the voice of a hijacker:

> "Uh, ...is the captain. Would like you all to remain seated. There is a bomb on board and are going back to the airport."

— **9:41 a.m.:** Cleveland Center loses United 93's transponder signal, but uses visual sightings from other planes to track its turn east, then south.

9:42 a.m.: FAA Command Center learns from television reports that a plane has struck the Pentagon. The FAA orders all airborne aircraft to land at the nearest airport.

9:45 a.m.: The White House is evacuated.

9:46 a.m.: Command Center notifies FAA headquarters that United 93 was 29 minutes away from Washington, D.C.

9:49 a.m.: FAA Command Center addresses Cleveland's 9:36 request to seek military intervention of United 93.

> **Command Center:** "Uh, do we want to think about, uh, scrambling aircraft?"
>
> **FAA Headquarters:** "Uh, God, I don't know."
>
> **Command Center:** "Uh, that's a decision somebody's gonna have to make probably in the next 10 minutes."

9:57 a.m.: President Bush departs Florida for Barksdale Air Force Base in Louisiana.

10:01 a.m.: Command Center tells FAA headquarters that another aircraft had seen United 93 "waving his wings." It's believed to be evidence of the passengers' efforts to overpower the hijackers.

10:03 a.m.: United Airlines Flight 93, en route from Newark, N.J., to San Francisco with 38 passengers, two pilots and five flight attendants aboard, crashes about 60 miles southeast of Pittsburgh.

10:05 a.m.: The south tower of the World Trade Center collapses.

10:10 a.m.: Part of the Pentagon collapses.

10:13 a.m.: The 39-story United Nations building is evacuated. A total of 11,700 people were evacuated "as a precautionary measure," a U.N. spokeswoman said.

10:24 a.m.: The FAA announces that all inbound trans-Atlantic aircraft into the United States are being diverted to Canada.

10:28 a.m.: The World Trade Center's north tower collapses from the top down.

- **10:45 a.m.:** All federal office buildings in Washington are evacuated.

- **10:52 a.m.:** Washington-area airports are reported closed by a Federal Aviation Administration spokeswoman.

- **11:02 a.m.:** New York City Mayor Rudy Giuliani orders the evacuation of the area south of the World Trade Center.

- **11:18 a.m.:** American Airlines says it has lost two planes. The airline says American Flight 11, a Boeing 767, en route from Boston to Los Angeles, and Flight 77, a Boeing 757 flying from Dulles Airport to San Francisco, have crashed.

- **11:26 a.m.:** United Airlines announces the crash of United Flight 93 southeast of Pittsburgh.

- **11:59 a.m.:** United Airlines confirms that Flight 175 has crashed with 56 passengers and nine crew members aboard.

- **1:04 p.m.:** President Bush, speaking from Barksdale Air Force Base, Louisiana, says the military has been put on high alert worldwide. He asks for prayers for those killed or wounded in the attacks: "Make no mistake, the United States will hunt down and punish those responsible for these cowardly acts."

- **1:48 p.m.:** President Bush leaves Barksdale aboard Air Force One and flies to Offutt Air Force Base in Omaha, Nebraska.

- **5:20 p.m.:** World Trade Center Tower 7 collapses.

- **6:41 p.m.:** Defense Secretary Donald Rumsfeld holds a news conference at the Pentagon. Rumsfeld announces the Pentagon will reopen for business.

- **6:54 p.m.:** President Bush returns to the White House from Omaha.

- **7:15 p.m.:** In a White House briefing, Attorney General John Ashcroft says:

    "We will not tolerate such acts."

- **8:30 p.m.:** President Bush addresses the nation from the Oval Office.

From the cockpit

"I was not working, but my wife was in a plane on the ground in Boston. She called me saying there was a big delay. I turned on the TV and saw the second plane hit the Twin Towers. I was almost in disbelief." ∎

The passengers and crewmembers on the airplanes lost on 9/11 are considered to be reminders of ultimate sacrifice. Many of them died acting heroically to save others. Below is a list of the airline employees who died on September 11th, 2001.

American 11 (Boston to Los Angeles) hit the World Trade Center.

John Ogonowski, Dracut, Mass. Captain

Thomas McGuinness, Portsmouth, N.H. First Officer

Barbara Arestegui; flight attendant

Jeffrey Collman, flight attendant

Sara Low, flight attendant

Karen Martin, flight attendant

Kathleen Nicosia, flight attendant

Betty Ong, flight attendant

Jean Roger, flight attendant

Dianne Snyder, flight attendant

Madeline Sweeney, flight attendant

United 175 (Boston to Los Angeles) crashed into World Trade Center.

Victor J. Saracini, Lower Makefield Township, Pa., Captain

Michael Horrocks, First Officer

Amy Jarret, flight attendant

Al Marchand, flight attendant

Amy King, flight attendant

Kathryn Laborie, flight attendant

Michael Tarrou, flight attendant

Alicia Titus, flight attendant

American 77 (Washington/Dulles to Los Angeles) crashed into the Pentagon.

Charles Burlingame, Captain

David Charlebois, First Officer

Michele Heidenberger, flight attendant

Jennifer Lewis, flight attendant

Kenneth Lewis, flight attendant

Renee May, flight attendant

United 93 (Newark to San Francisco) crashed in Shanksville, Pennsylvania.

Jason Dahl, Colorado, Captain

Leroy Homer, Marlton, N.J., First Officer

Sandy Bradshaw, flight attendant

CeeCee Lyles, flight attendant

Lorraine Bay, flight attendant

Wanda Green, flight attendant

Deborah Welsh, flight attendant

In the aftermath of the attack, it took four days before airline flights began again. Some crewmembers refused to fly because they didn't feel there was enough security in place to protect them. With four 9/11 airliners hijacked and destroyed in a single day, no one could blame them.

Those who braved the return to work entered a very different workplace.

From the cockpit

"I was back flying a few days after 9/11. It was strange to see the terminals so empty and the planes even emptier. We had two people in first class and three in coach on a plane that could hold several hundred passengers. The first officer would place the cockpit crash axe in his lap (Yes, we carry a razor sharp axe in the cockpit.), and before a flight attendant could enter the flight deck another flight attendant would barricade the area in front of the door with a galley cart to slow down any attempt to breach the cockpit. Only then, could the flight attendant on the cockpit side of the barricade enter the flight deck. Needless to say getting a cup of coffee was an ordeal." ■

As airline crews returned to the skies, a new danger was posed: layoffs. On September 15, 2001, Continental Airlines released a statement that it would cut 12,000 jobs. One by one, other airlines followed. United and American announced 20,000 layoffs each; US Airways 11,000; Northwest, 10,000; and Delta had pink slips for 13,000. The layoff toll topped 140,000.

From the cockpit

"On the morning of 9/11, I was flying from Las Vegas to Memphis. As we arrived at the aircraft, one of the mechanics came up to the cockpit and told us that a plane had flown into the World Trade Center. We discussed what might happen, then prepared for departure. We taxied to the end of the runway and were ready for takeoff. The plane in front of us took off, so we were next. After sitting there for several minutes, we told the air traffic controller that we were ready. His response was: 'Hold on. We have a hold on all traffic.'" ■

The 9/11 tragedy hit the airline industry hard, but it also accelerated airline rule and structure changes already underway. These changes have made flying safer for everyone today.

 ***Fast Fact***

The two skyscrapers of the World Trade Center destroyed on 9/11 were also called the Twin Towers. They looked just alike and were over 1,360 feet tall each.[13]

The Miracle on the Hudson

Not all aviation failures end in tragedy. It is such a safe industry with highly-trained pilots that common accidents are usually avoided. Sometimes, the professional and expert training of a pilot can even avoid a terrible crash against miraculous odds.

---

13. Skyscraper, n.d.

On January 15, 2009, US Airways Flight 1549 departed from LaGuardia Airport in Queens, New York, just like any other normal day. Shortly after takeoff, the aircraft suffered bird strikes in both engines. The Airbus A320-214 lost thrust rapidly, but instead of crashing, the crew was able to ditch the plane safely into the Hudson River. All 107 passengers aboard the aircraft survived.

 **Fast Fact**

A "bird strike" is a term for the common event of a bird and an airplane colliding. Bird strikes can happen at any time on the taxiways, runways, or in the air.

The captain of US Airways Flight 1549 was Captain Chesley Burnett Sullenberger III. His friends called him "Sully." Captain Sully had years of experience flying airplanes. Before he was a commercial airline pilot, he was a fighter pilot in the military.

All of this experience became important about one and a half minutes after the airplane took off from the LaGuardia runway and crossed paths with a flock of Canadian geese. The collision with the birds took out both engines. The engines lost all of their power and left Captain Sully with no choice but to make an emergency landing.

 **Fast Fact**

Thrust is the name of the force that makes an airplane move through the air.

Air Traffic Control told the captain and his flight crew to fly the plane to Teterboro Airport in New Jersey. There was one problem. Flight 1549 was in such bad shape it wasn't possible for the airplane to make it back to any airport, not even one closer than LaGuardia. Captain Sully told ATC that he would not be able to make it. "We're going to be in the Hudson," he advised them.

 **Fast Fact**

The "Miracle on the Hudson" event took place in only five minutes and 36 seconds, from the time Flight 1549 took off from LaGuardia to when it landed in the Hudson River in eastern New York.

Below are parts of the actual tense but calm conversations that occurred between Captain Sully and air traffic controllers that day. You may notice in this official transcript that sometimes the pilots and air traffic controllers misidentified Flight 1549, mixing up the last number. One can imagine this was because of nerves!

Abbreviated Key

AWE1549 (Cactus): US AIRWAYS 1549

LGA: La Guardia Tower

ATCI L116: New York TRACON

LaGuardia Departure TEB: Teterboro ATC

Transcript

3:24:54: [Flight 1549 is cleared for takeoff.]

3:26:00 (L116): *Cactus 1549, New York departure radar contact. Climb and maintain 15,000.*

3:26:04 (AWE1549): *Maintain 15,000, 1549.*

3:27:32 (L116): *Cactus 1549, turn left heading 270.*

3:27:36 (AWE1549): *Ah, this is, uh, Cactus 1549. Hit birds, we lost thrust in both engines. We're turning back toward LaGuardia.*

3:27:42 (L116): *Okay, yea, you need to return to LaGuardia. Turn left heading of, uh, 220.*

3:27:46 (AWE1549): *220.*

3:27:49 (L116): *Tower, stop your departures. We got an emergency landing.*

3:27:53 (LGA): *Who is it?*

3:27:54 (L116): *It's 1529. He, ah, bird strike. He lost all engines. He lost the thrust in the engines. He is returning immediately.*

3:27:59 (LGA): *Cactus 1529, which engines?*

3:28:01 (L116): *He lost thrust in both engines, he said.*

3:28:03 (LGA): *Got it.*

3:28:05 (L116): *Cactus 1529, if we can get it, do you want to try to land Runway 13?*

3:28:11 (AWE1549): *We're unable. We may end up in the Hudson.*

3:28:31 (L116): *Alright, Cactus 1549, it's going to be left traffic to Runway 31.*

3:28:34 (AWE154): *Unable.*

3:28:36 (L116): *Okay, what do you need to land?*

3:28:46 (L116): *Cactus 1549, Runway 49-- Runway 4 is available if you want to make left traffic to Runway 4.*

3:28:50 (AWE1549): *I'm not sure if we can make any runway. Oh, what's over to our right? Anything in New Jersey? Maybe Teterboro?*

3:28:55 (L116): *Okay, yea, off to your right side is Teterboro Airport.*

3:29:02 (L116): *Do you want to try and go to Teterboro?*

3:29:03 (AWE1549): *Yes.*

3:29:05 (L116): *Teterboro, Empire-- actually LaGuardia Departure got an emergency inbound.*

3:29:10 (TEB): *Okay, go ahead.*

3:29:11 (L116): *Cactus 1529 over the George Washington Bridge, wants to go to the airport right now.*

3:29:14 (TEB): *He wants to go to our airport, check. Does he need any assistance?*

3:29:17 (L116): *Ah, yes. He, ah, he was a bird strike. Can I get him in for Runway 1?*

3:29:19 (TEB): *Runway 1, that's good.*

3:29:21 (L116): *Cactus 1529, turn right 280. You can land Runway 1 at Teterboro.*

3:29:25 (AWE1549): *We can't do it.*

3:29:26 (L116): *Okay, which runway would you like at Teterboro?*

3:29:28 (AWE1549): *We're gonna be in the Hudson.*

3:29:33 (L116): *I'm sorry, say again, Cactus.*

3:29:51 (L116): *Cactus, ah, Cactus 1549, radar contact is lost. You also got Newark Airport off your two o'clock and about 7 miles.*

3:30:14 (L116): *Cactus 1529, uh, you still on?*

3:30:22 (L116): *Cactus 1529, if you can, ah, you got, ah, Runway 29 available at Newark off your two o'clock and 7 miles.*

3:30:30: Splashdown. The radar and tower notified the Coast Guard who responded: *We launched the fleet.*

Captain Sully had no engine power. He could not fly, but he could glide. He guided Flight 1549 into the Hudson River and hoped that the plane would not break-up on impact. Luckily, it landed in one piece with a bumpy, dangerous splash. Fortunately, the aircraft floated on the top of the water long enough for all of the passengers and crew to exit out onto the wings or into the water with life vests.

Captain Sully searched the plane twice before exiting last. Of the survivors, only one injury was serious. Although it was winter and the water was freezing, the fast response from rescue boats and ferries prevented any deaths.

After the incident, Captain Sully and his crew were cleared of any responsibility for the accident. The governor of New York praised him and called the close call the "Miracle on the Hudson". The name stuck.

From the cockpit

"A bad day for me is when the weather is bad. Things like snow, ice, and thunderstorms require a lot more concentration. They also cause delays, which mean it takes more time to accomplish the mission." ∎

Captain Sullenberger received many honors and awards, including an invitation to the swearing in of President Barack Obama. In 2016, a movie about the accident starring Tom Hanks was released. Sully retired from US Airways and published a book about his life.

CHAPTER 7

Peak of the Profession

The Pilot's Lifestyle

Becoming a pilot means living an unusual lifestyle. It's not only a respected career, everyday people think it's glamorous and an easy way to make a high salary. The truth is, pilots are everyday people, too, who just happen to have a job that takes years of training and has some unique advantages. In reality, it's just as tough as any other job, although it may affect people in different ways than other jobs.

Many people interested in becoming a commercial airline pilot wonder about where they should live. Research and surveys usually come up with different answers, but living outside of a major city is a common expectation. That isn't always the case, though.

 ## *Fast Fact*

The most populated city in the United States is New York City. Three major airports service this area: John F. Kennedy (JFK – Queens, NY), La Guardia (LGA – Queens, NY), and Newark (EWR – Newark, NJ).

Some pilots live in cities with regional jets that can fly them to work at a major airport. For example, a pilot that flies out of the Atlanta-Hartsfield Airport in Georgia could live in the nearby city of Savannah and take a short flight to Atlanta to fly an aircraft for work several times across the country before returning home.

There are also pilots who live near large airports but fly out of them to work in other states. It's common for a pilot who does not want to leave his big city hometown to do just that. One example would be a pilot living in Atlanta flying to Dallas, Texas, in the morning and flying an aircraft from Texas to different destinations as his day job. Some of the more popular states to live in for pilots are Texas, Florida, and California.[14]

Rags to riches

As explained in previous chapters, captains make more money than first officers and other members of the flight crew. A lot more money. To be precise, the average pay for a "jumbo jet" captain can reach $270,000 per year.[15]

The big gap between captains who make that much and first officers who barely make minimum wage has been blamed for the decline of available commercial pilots over the years. Even pilots who learn to fly in the mili-

---

14. Kolmar, 2016
15. Airline Pilot Central, 2017

tary at the expense of the government must begin their commercial airline career at the bottom of seniority with low wages.

From the cockpit

"Many years ago I was called from the flight deck to defuse a drunken brawl between several first class passengers. I put on my coat and hat before leaving the cockpit, hoping the authority figure presence of 'yours truly' would help. The entire first class section listened as I calmly explained what I was going to do if the drunken individuals did not remain quietly in their seats for the duration of the flight. The threat of being arrested upon landing seemed to get most of their attention. Satisfied things were under control, I turned back toward the cockpit but felt a tug on my coat sleeve. I looked down and saw a well-dressed man motioning to speak with me. I leaned down and he whispered, 'How come you're so calm?' I simply answered, 'That's what I get paid for.'" ■

Dealing with low income in the beginning of a commercial piloting career is a challenge, and it definitely affects your lifestyle. Money is tight in those first few years as a major airline pilot. It's a fact of life, but if you want to fly big jets with hopes of a big retirement income, you will have to pay your dues. It's not uncommon for junior captains at smaller carriers to have less experience than their military trained first or second officers. However, over time, that usually becomes meaningless, especially at the major airlines where, with rare exception, the person in the captain's seat is usually the most qualified to be there.

Hobbies

Just as in any other high stress career, pilots find it's important to have hobbies when they are not at the airport or in an aircraft. In the past, airline managers and **flight surgeons**, (the health care providers for aviation careers,) insisted it was best for pilots to do nothing but rest between airline trips. Eventually, they realized pilots who had hobbies were in better health both physically and mentally.

 ## *Fast Fact*

A flight surgeon is the term for the medical doctor that gives pilots and air traffic controllers a yearly medical examination to determine if they're physically fit to fly or work airplanes. This physical include vision tests, hearing checks, and periodic heart monitoring called EKG.

Although traveling and meeting all kinds of people could be fun, the industry began to encourage pilots to find new hobbies, especially if they were relaxing.

 ## *From the cockpit*

"After leveling off at cruise altitude, it was over an hour before the lead flight attendant called the cockpit to see if we needed anything. I inquired who the first class passengers were, and she said something like, 'We have comedians Tim Conway and Don Knotts sitting in First.' I grew up laughing at the on-screen antics of both of these gentlemen — they were two of the funniest people on the planet. I asked the flight attendent if she'd invite the comics to the cockpit when we landed in Detroit — surprisingly they jumped at the chance.

"It was nearing midnight when we landed in Detroit. Once at the gate, the airplane emptied within seconds. After responding to the Parking Check List, I opened the cockpit door and looked directly at Tim Conway and Don Knotts waiting patiently with big smiles, outwardly excited to visit the cockpit. After a brief handshake I invited them to both climb up front and sit in the pilots' seats. For me, the rest is show biz legend. I spent the next 20 minutes entertained by the two funniest and 'real-people' celebrities I have ever encountered — and there have been many." ■

The hobbies that pilots and others in aviation enjoy aren't much different than the activities everyone else likes to do. It all depends on the person and what he or she finds relaxing. Some pilots enjoy building model airplanes; others like to work on cars. There is music, trap shooting, collectibles, writing, and even sports. Depending on where a pilot lives, many people get their scuba certification so they can dive at different locations on trips around the country or the world.

 **Fast Fact**

According to Forbes magazine, in 2017 some of the most popular hobbies include gardening, art, design, pets, travel, reading, writing, cooking, shopping, health, and fitness. [16]

Health

When it comes to being a commercial airline pilot, you may want to pay close attention to your health. Some studies say pilots live longer than av-

---

16. Forbes, 2017

erage, but those numbers show they are about pilots who retire at around 60-years-old. Other research has concluded that pilots, especially those who fly internationally, do not live as long as the rest of the population.

Is it skipping meals or bad food choices? Could it be the irregular sleeping hours? All of these reasons could play a part, but the most important thing to remember is that a good diet and regular exercise go a long way for everyone.

 **_Fast Fact_**

A 2001 health survey found pilots have a higher rate of melanoma, a type of skin cancer, than the rest of the general population.[17]

Besides encouraging hobbies, airline managers and even the FAA are also concerned about pilot health, especially those who are overweight. People who are obese are more likely to suffer from **Obstructive Sleep Apnea (OSA)**. This health issue interferes with a regular, normal sleep cycle which leaves a person exhausted. Worse, OSA can cause someone to fall asleep suddenly without any warning and at any time.

Although a pilot cannot be fired for being obese, airlines encourage a healthy lifestyle and an understanding of how to calculate the ideal body weight for their health.

 **_Fast Fact_**

Body fat is measured and based on weight and height. Today, doctors use Body Mass Index or BMI, to determine a person's ideal healthy weight. BMI is a chart which shows the ideal weight for a person's age and height.

---

17. Butler, 2001

Relationships

Relationships take a great deal of work. For pilots, a relationship or marriage can be difficult because of long hours away from home. It can be hard for family and friends to understand what it's like to fly for long hours and eat and sleep away from home. Pilots say a commercial airline career is not as glamorous as most people think it is because of the loneliness and fatigue.

From the cockpit

"My wife and I travel, go to the beach, and visit our kids and grandkids." ■

Divorce in the United States runs high. In 2015, there were about 17 divorces for every 1,000 couples.[18] According to some aviation experts, the divorce rate is as high as 75% for pilots.[19] Because of their unusual careers, pilots have to be aware of the cost of their jobs as well as their own personality types and how they maintain lifelong relationships. This doesn't mean that every pilot is in an unhappy relationship or divorced. There are many happy families in aviation. In fact, some pilots have spouses or children who are also pilots, flight attendants, or work in air traffic.

Retirement: What to Expect

As of 2017, the FAA requires all commercial airline pilots to retire before their 65th birthday. If that sounds unusual, it's because it is. There aren't many careers that have a required retirement age.

---

18. Time, 2016
19. Airline Pilot Central, 2014

From the cockpit

"Thousands of pilots will reach the mandatory retirement age during the next 10 years, so now is a great time to become a pilot." ■

Pilots used to receive **pensions** from the airlines they worked for, but it cost the airlines a lot of money to save the money for them to receive later. Today, pilots are on their own for saving up to live after they can no longer fly. Most pilots save money that will grow during the years in a **401K** account. Airlines do provide benefits packages that will put money in a pilot's 401K, so that helps.

Fast Fact

Benefit packages are bonuses besides the regular salary that an employee may receive. Most benefits include health insurance, retirement plans, and options in the event the employee becomes disabled.

Another reason pilots plan their own retirement options today is because using an airline's benefits alone can be risky. If a pilot loses his job, he can lose his retirement with the company, too. When an airline goes bankrupt, most of the time the pilots lose the retirement that they've saved up with the company.

From the cockpit

"I was fortunate to work for a company with a great retirement plan. We had a pension plan and a 401K plan. Since I am retired and living in Florida, we are planning to buy a boat this year for fishing and recreational boating. Generally, I'm just relaxing and enjoying the good life." ■

Many pilots do have a second job. Some find it necessary to get a different job after they retire as a pilot if their retirement plans don't work out.

 **Fast Fact**

Flight dispatchers work for different airlines. They plan the flights, observe weather, and calculate fuels along with different load weights. Retired pilots have enough experience to be flight dispatchers.

Even after a pilot retires from flying, he or she can still work for an airline doing a different job. Some retired captains give flight lessons, train new pilots in computer simulators, or act as managers for airlines or airports. A retired pilot can also work for the NTSB and investigate accidents. Some become professors and teach aviation. Others are entering the drone market as drone operators.

From the cockpit

"My wife wanted to know if I wanted a [retirement] party or for her to accompany me on the last trip. I chose none of this, preferring to leave, just as I initially came into the airline industry — quietly and unnoticed. Checking in, I tried to downplay my quiet exit, but a clerk I had known for years actually came out to the plane with a tearful hug and goodbye as I sat slightly embarrassed in the captain's seat.

When she left the cockpit my first officer said, 'What's up with that, boss?' Needless to say, I informed him of the situation, but asked that he keep the fact quiet. On the last leg home, it was not my turn to fly the leg, but the first officer kindly said, 'You got this one boss — make it count.'

It was a cool crisp late afternoon as I smoothly landed the nearly full Boeing 757-300 for the last time. The landing gods must have been with me because I never felt the wheels touch the ground. I rolled the entire length of the runway savoring these last moments. I was one with the plane — we were a single unit performing a ballet I had practiced all my life. As I turned off at the runway, my eyes moistened. That was the last time I would ever land a commercial airliner — and the reality was sinking in.

The taxi from the end of the runway to the gate was the longest I ever remember. There were flashbacks of thousands of flights in my thoughts; some funny, some heartbreaking. Each of those countless trips taught me lessons about myself, but more importantly, they brought me close to many talented people I was honored to fly and work with. As the arena of gates, planes, and ground equipment swept behind me, I eased the 250,000-pound airliner into my final gate.

The crew presented me with a signed good-bye card and as the 200 plus passengers exited the plane, I shook hands with each and every one saying, 'Thank you for the privilege,' and indeed it had been." ∎

CHAPTER 8

Flight Today

The Major Airlines

Travel websites and businesses will argue about which airline in the United States is actually the best, but the top three airline companies by size[20] and operations today are considered to be:

American Airlines

Delta Airlines

Southwest Airlines

American Airlines

The airline known for its connection to aviation pioneer Charles Lindberg, American Airlines delivered mail in 1926 with Lindberg in the cockpit. The route from St. Louis, Missouri, to Chicago, Illinois, ran for eight years.

---

20. Deglmann, 2017

By the 1930s, passengers took over the space once for letters and packages, and American began passenger service from Chicago to New York at the end of the decade.

The headquarters for American Airlines is in Fort Worth, Texas. The company has **hubs** in some of the country's biggest cities: Chicago, Miami, Los Angeles, and New York. It provides flights to about 50 different countries, with about 6,700 flights a day. That's a lot of air traffic for the ready pilot.

American employs about 14,000 airline pilots. As of 2017, the company is looking to hire about 750 more.[21] There are hundreds of other jobs with this company. As of 2016, American employed thousands of ticket agents, gate agents, ramp agents, mechanics, and other personnel.

---

21. Airline Pilot Central, n.d.

The airline holds the unfortunate record for greatest loss of life in an airline crash. It happened on May 25, 1979, when American Airlines Flight 191 took off from Chicago for a trip to Los Angeles. Just after takeoff, the DC-10 lost an engine. The aircraft flipped, fell to the earth, and exploded into hot flames that left nothing intact.

Today American Airlines is the largest airline since it joined with US Airways in 2015 to become the biggest in the world. It posted $40 million of revenue in 2016.

Delta

Delta Air Lines began as a Macon, Georgia, crop-dusting business in 1924. Named the Huff Daland Dusters, the small planes dropped chemicals over farms or other agricultural businesses. It soon became international, dusting crops as far away as South America.

In 1928, the company was bought by C. E. Woolman and named Delta Air Service. Within a year, Delta began flying passengers back and forth between Texas and Mississippi. Only five passengers and a pilot could fit on the small Travel Air S-6000B airplane in those early days.

Today, Delta headquarters is in Atlanta, Georgia. It has hubs in major cities like Seattle, Washington, Los Angeles, California, Salt Lake City, Utah, and New York. The company has about 80,000 employees.[22] It flies over 15,000 flights every day to over 62 countries.

---

22. Delta, 2017

The most infamous event involving Delta Air Lines happened in 1985. Eerily, it has the same flight number as the 1979 American Airlines tragedy. In this case, Delta Air Lines Flight 191 departed from Fort Lauderdale, Florida, for a flight to Dallas, Texas. Just before landing, the aircraft made contact with a microburst of air and was pushed into the ground a mile short of the airport runway. Of the 152 passengers aboard, 128 lost their lives.

 ### *Did you know*

The term "wind shear" is often confused with the word, "microburst," although they are two different things. Wind shear is a change or variation in wind speed from any direction that can apply a great deal of force. A microburst, on the other hand, is another strong air current, but it is usually sudden, in one spot, and occurs as a down draft. Both events are sometimes linked to airline accidents. Pilots are trained to deal with these phenomena.

Today Delta is in the top 20 of the world's safest airlines with Australia's Quantas leading the pack. It has a reputation of being generous to its employees. In 2016, Delta was named one of Fortune 100's Best Places to Work For.[23] The company posted it made over $6 billion in profit before taxes that same year. Half of that was returned to **shareholders**. They had a total of $39.6 billion in sales.

Southwest Airlines

Rounding out the top three of the biggest airlines in the United States is Southwest Airlines. Southwest is a younger airline than American and Delta. This company had a slow beginning but crept to the front of the pack by providing personal service. Rollin King and Herb Kelleher created it in 1967. The first flights were in Texas between Dallas, Houston, and San Antonio.

23. Kruse, 2017

During the 1980s, Southwest ranked number one in customer service. Passengers loved the discounts and an air miles program that gave points for free flights. By 1998, it ranked number five in the United States.

Southwest keeps its headquarters in Dallas, Texas. It employed over 53,000 workers, including pilots, by 2016. It posted over $20 billion in sales and $2.2 billion in profits. It was also ranked #35 of the best companies to work for by Forbes in the same year.[24]

One interesting fact about Southwest Airlines is that it has an impressive history of safety. The company has never had any major airplane crashes. However, it was involved in a death in 2005 when one of its planes slid off a runway in snowy conditions and struck three cars. One of the young occupants in the cars did not survive.

These days, Southwest Airlines operates over 3,900 flights per day with 8,600 pilots. It flies to about 101 destinations in eight different countries.[25] Southwest is looking to the future, planning flights to popular destinations such as Hawaii, Alaska, and Canada, as the company grows.

Technology and Advancements

Aviation technology is moving just as fast as advancements in other related fields. Pilots today are seeing improvements and computer programing that give them more advantages than ever before. In the cockpit especially, science is moving at great speeds in more ways than one.

24. Forbes, 2017
25. SWAMedia, 2017

From the cockpit

"Aircraft cockpits changed a lot in the years that I flew. Engines are a lot more reliable, aircraft systems are more reliable, and the electronics have become more sophisticated. In the future, cockpits will become more and more computerized and automated." ■

Some of the new tools pilots are finding in commercial aircraft make it easier to navigate and see. Just like the displays used in the military, commercial airline pilots now have access to **Heads Up Displays (HUDS).** These display shows important information pilots need to know in order to fly the airplane. The information such as speed and altitude is projected on the windshield in front of the pilot. They can "look through" the information and see the outside world, then back to the screen without missing important details. Some of the data found on cockpit HUDS can be warnings for wind shears or information to help the pilot avoid collisions, both in the air or on the runways.

Another new program creating a stir in technology is Smart Taxi, which has a multi-functional display. Using GPS, this program allows a pilot to see a map of the runways and taxiways of an airport from the cockpit. This is especially useful if the pilot is new to the airport. The map not only shows what's all around him or her, it shows the airplane as it moves along the routes ordered by air traffic control.

Technology is helping build better airplanes, too. Airbus has turned to the amazing technology of 3D printing. In fact, the company uses 3D printing to make over 1,000 of the parts that go on its A350.[26] This type of advancement is most popular for spare parts, but its use is growing. Aviation tools are being "printed" which is less expensive and easier for some of the more

26. Wong, 2016

complicated instruments. Another advantage is that these aircraft parts and tools are lighter!

 ## Fast Fact

The marvel of 3D printing was invented by an American named Chuck Hull in 1983. The first object he printed was a tiny cup.

A new virtual reality headset is helping to train beginner pilots. Rather than sit in a simulator, students sit in front of a computer with a pair of goggles. The goggles give the wearer a real life but virtual view inside and outside of the cockpit, so they can practice flying a plane without having to get in a simulator or the real thing. Virtual reality training saves costs on classrooms, travel, and the need to pay a large number of instructors.

Bigger and faster

It's not just the cockpit that's getting a new makeover. Aviation manufacturers are building planes bigger and faster. In Russia and Asia, the new manufacturing company China-Russia Commercial Aircraft International Corporation (CRAIC) is working on a 280-passenger airplane that will compete with large airliners built by Boeing and Airbus. The aircraft, called the C929, will be a wide-body model with two rows of aisles.[27] Technology will provide it with advanced programs and systems to save fuel and lives.

The United States military is also looking ahead. A new stealth jet is in the works to be a part of future Air Force programs.[28] This new aircraft will carry a human pilot that can release and guide groups of drones that fly with the help of turbo fans.

---

27. Polek, 2017
28. Scout, 2017

Cutting down on human pilots and replacing them with robots is one way to save lives. However, some experts feel too much technology isn't a good thing. Robots and computers cannot feel or respond the way a human pilot can. On the other hand, a robot can handle more **gravitational force** than the human body.

The military has also turned to lasers. As of 2017, a successful laser test was conducted in New Mexico at the White Sands Missile Range with an Apache military helicopter. The laser used a targeting program to stay on its target until it was able to successfully fire. Future tests include using lasers on moving targets. However, more research needs to be done because lasers don't work well in smoky, clouded air.

From the cockpit

"The military is going toward more and more drones because it takes pilots out of harm's way, and you can keep a drone up in the air a lot longer than a pilot can stay awake. Plus, it is much cheaper to make and train a drone than a pilot." ∎

Drones are also advancing in speed and accuracy. Some experts predict a drone may someday replace military and commercial airline pilots altogether. A drone is a robotic unmanned aircraft. It can be small enough to fit in your hand or as large as an aircraft that you'd expect to find a pilot inside. Drones work using onboard programs with GPS, sensors, and other aviation requirements needed to fly and think.

From the cockpit

"Aircraft are becoming more and more automated and complex, but I feel we are still 40 to 50 years away from self-flying airplanes. For a company like Airbus or Boeing to manufacture a new airplane and get it certified by the FAA, it can take as long as seven to 10 years before it's on an airline's property. This of course depends on many factors, but it will be years before we see drones flying around passengers." ■

Passenger perks

Technology is changing for the passengers that fly on airplanes, too. Today it is not necessary to stand in long lines at a ticket counter. Tickets can be purchased on the internet and printed off. They can even be stored on a smart phone with a barcode.

Another new advancement is beacon technology. This form of positioning system was created for situations where GPS won't work. Using a GPS can be tough indoors, and that can make it hard for passengers to move around inside an airport. With beacon technology, people can receive personal information like changed gate numbers, the location of their favorite bar and grill, and where to find their bags once they've been taken off of the airplane. It's personalized positioning for the modern traveler.

 ***Fast Fact***

Airline passengers say they are willing to spend up to as much as $100 on onboard purchases like movies, Wi-Fi, meals, and alcohol.[29]

Looking ahead, travelers can look forward to a new, but strange technology being adapted for eye tracking. This future advance will add convenience to passengers watching movies on in-flight monitors. The program tracks the viewer's eyes and pauses the movie or other form of media when he or she looks away. That way a passenger can order a drink or get up to use the restroom without ever having to hit the pause button.[30]

Now, that's service!

Pilots of the Future

Will technology get rid of the commercial pilot? Not anytime soon. Technology continues to make flying easier and safer as long as that technology works. There is a huge need for pilots now, and the demand for them is expected to continue for the next 10 years.

Pilots agree that now is a great time to choose aviation as a career and find a job with a successful airline. As more and more captains reach retirement age, there will be career and schedule changes that will open doors for a young or new pilot.

29. Winton, 2016
30. Wong, 2016

From the cockpit

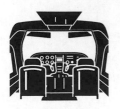

"The requirement for having a flight engineer has already gone by the wayside during my career. However, with the issues of having [terrorists] intentionally crash planes, I am guessing we won't see single pilot cockpits any time soon. I know airline CEOs who would like to have no pilots." ∎

The growing concern for the shortage of available, qualified pilots in the aviation industry has created a lot of questions. Young people interested in aviation want and need to know if becoming a commercial airline pilot is the best career choice. Fortunately, retired pilots are anxious to pass on their knowledge and see the industry grow.

From the cockpit

"I don't see drones taking over or even entering passenger travel. There is so much that pilots do that it's not possible to do it with a camera in a trailer in some desert." ∎

It is true that the military is using fewer and fewer pilots with advanced drones. This sends some would-be military pilots to the airlines. This is good for the industry. It is busy looking ahead and trying to figure out how to best train and prepare pilots for the near future.

From the cockpit

"Occasionally, you hear about someone wanting to make a pilot-less aircraft. I personally don't see that happening for quite a while. I believe that the career of the professional pilot will be a good choice for a long time into the future." ∎

The airline industry is also working on improving opportunities and pay for new pilots. They are trying to find aviators who have the "right stuff" and who would make excellent captains in the cockpit.

It's an important message to understand. While technology has improved, the commercial airline pilot is still needed in the left seat.

From the cockpit

"I don't think we will see remotely piloted commercial aircraft for a while. Too much goes on with weather and passenger issues to be able to react with current technology." ∎

Women can also take heart. They are at a new advantage. Female pilots have become important factors in aviation now because they are exciting options for the concern over pilot shortages. There was only one in over 21,000 women with a pilot certificate in 1960. In the 1980s, that number had jumped to one in a little over 4,000. However, despite this improvement, meeting a female commercial airline pilot can be rare. Many feel it's time for that to change.

From the cockpit

"Pay is going up because pilot demand is going up and there are not very many people willing to enter this industry due to the steep entrance fees. I don't see that continuing. Airlines are working hard to get the 1,500 hours experience rule changed." ∎

So, is a commercial airline pilot career the one for you? It may be if you have the passion, commitment, and patience. Pilots are respected for their dependability, self-control, attention to detail, and ability to manage stress. Yes, it takes money, time, and experience, but the left seat is available to anyone who is willing to work for the dream.

So, the next time you see a captain or first officer standing at the doorway saying goodbye to passengers, take a moment to shake his or her hand and thank them for the safe trip. It's what they get paid to do for you, and they've worked hard for the privilege. No matter where a pilot is on the ladder of the commercial airline pilot career, a captain still likes knowing that you care. After all, you may be standing in their shoes someday.

Author's Note

It's a bird! It's a plane! It's an author!

You may be wondering if the writer of this book has actually flown an airplane. The answer to that good question is, no, but I have flown as a passenger inside many types of aircraft to places all over the United States and Caribbean.

Flight as a means of adventure has always been a part of my life. With family and friends working in the aviation field, I get to talk, hang out, or work with flight attendants, gate agents, ramp agents, air traffic controllers, and pilots all the time.

This book is a revised edition of *This is Your Captain: The Naked Truth About the Person Flying Your Plane* by Captain Jack Watson. It is especially for young and new adult readers, as well as anyone interested in checking out a career as a commercial airline pilot.

Dreams take courage and a heck of a lot of hard work. That's all you really need to know to become an airline pilot or anything else you want to be. I hope this book helps you open the door with an understanding of what to do next. Best of luck as you begin your journey.

Danielle Thorne

Acknowledgements

This book is a revised edition of *This is Your Captain: The Naked Truth About the Person Flying Your Plane* by Captain Jack Watson. It has been written especially for young adults or anyone interested in a career as a commercial airline pilot.

Captain Watson's knowledge and experiences were invaluable in organizing ideas and chapters into a fun and easy-to-read book about this field. His information provided great selections and jumping off points for exploring many aspects of the career.

In addition and just as importantly, the depth and character of this book would not have been if it weren't for the many voices from the world of aviation that provided professional input and critiques of the actual day-to-day life of an airline pilot through interviews and emails.

While those many sources, including pilots and air traffic controllers, shared invaluable data to make this book as reliable and current as possible, most choose to remain anonymous as they are still on active duty. Otherwise, a huge *thank you* to Captain Gary Doby and Captain Mike Pfliger, the office staff at Atlantic Publishing, and my steady and reliable editor, Lisa McGinnes.

Cockpit Slang

Arm the doors: the pre-flight task to assure the door is secure and evacuation slides are armed

A/C: crew-speak for the aircraft

Add-on: normally refers to a flight attendant who was not listed on the flight schedule but was penciled in due to another calling in sick

Air pocket: transient jolt of turbulence

All-call: often part of the arming/disarming procedure, a request that each flight attendant report via intercom from his or her station — flight attendant conference call

Alley: a taxiway or passageway between terminals or **ramps**

Apron: similar to **ramp;** any expanse of **tarmac** not a runway or taxiway: i.e., areas where planes park or are serviced

Area of weather: typically a thunderstorm or a zone of heavy precipitation.

Base: flight crew term for their home airport; where their flights originate and terminate

Bid: when a pilot or flight attendant puts in a request for a specific route or schedule; usually done on a monthly basis

Bottle to throttle: curfew hours. In airline speak, the time a person must abstain from having another alcoholic beverage and the time of their next flight; often 12 hours

Commute: process of getting to starting destination or base. Pilots and flight attendants often live in one city but have another city as their base, and so *commute* to work

Crash pad: the term used by flight attendants and pilots in reference to a rented apartment, motel room or house usually shared by several flight attendants and or pilots

Crumb crunchers: a term flight attendants use in reference to children passengers

Deadhead: when a pilot or flight attendant flies as a passenger if it is part of their job

Deplane: used to describe the opposite of boarding an aircraft.

Direct flight: a routing along which the flight number does not change; has nothing to do with whether the plane stops

EFC time: expect further clearance (EFC) time; sometimes called a release time, the point in time where a crew expects to be set free from a **holding pattern** or a **ground stop**

Equipment: the airplane

F/A: flight attendant

Ferry flight an aircraft flies to a specific destination without paying passengers aboard

Final approach: when a plane has reached the last, straight-in segment of the landing pattern that is aligned with the extended centerline of the runway

First officer (also, copilot: second in command on the **flight deck**; fully qualified to operate the aircraft in all stages of flight, including takeoffs and landings.

Flight deck: the cockpit

Flight level: how many thousands of feet above sea level. Example: Flight level three-three zero is 33,000 feet

George: a colloquial term for "autopilot"

Green aircraft: slang term; a plane fresh from the factory with exterior paint and interior still incomplete

Ground stop: when departures to one or more destinations are stopped by ATC, usually due to air traffic congestion at the destination airport

Holding pattern: a racetrack-shaped course flown around an airport during weather or traffic delays

Illegal: pilot or flight attendant who crosses over the maximum hours allowed to work per flight, day, or schedule without a required sleep or break period

In range: somewhere around the start of descent, pilots send an electronic "in range" message to let everybody at the arrival station know they'll be arriving shortly

Interphone: the phones located throughout the cabin that allow flight attendants to speak with each other and the flight deck when the cockpit door is shut

Jump seat: a flight term referring to an auxiliary (extra) seat for persons who are not operating the aircraft.

Kettle class: a mocking term for economy or coach class, taken from the hillbilly characters.

Last minute paperwork: usually refers to last minute weight-and-balance corrections, a revision to the flight plan, or waiting for maintenance to deal with a write-up; all to get the logbook in order

Line: the schedule of trips a pilot or flight attendant is awarded after bid results are posted each month

Line holder: a pilot or flight attendant senior enough to hold a line and not be on reserve

Lounge lizard: a pilot or flight attendant who skips the use of a crash pad, choosing instead to sleep in the crew lounge at the airport, usually to save money

Narrowbody: a plane with one aisle down the center

Non-rev: short for "non-revenue;" identifies an airline employee or a family member who takes advantage of the company perks to fly at a nominal cost or for free free

Nonstop: flight that doesn't stop

Offline city: a city the airline or flight does not normally fly to

PAX: an abbreviation for "passengers."

Pre-board: refers to those passengers who board first and ahead of all first, business, and coach class passengers

Ramp: refers to the aircraft and ground vehicle movement areas closest to the terminal; the aircraft parking zones and surrounds

Tarmac: refers to any ramp, apron, or taxiway surface

Transcon: a transcontinental flight across one continent or country

Turn: a flight that leaves base and returns back to base in the same day; also known as a turnaround

Wheels-up time: similar to the **EFC time**, except it refers to the time when a ground-stopped plane is expected to be fully airborne

Widebody: a large plane with a row of seats going down the center, meaning there are two aisles in the main cabin

Z Time: Greenwich Mean Time, which is the time at the Royal Observatory in Greenwich, London; is not affected by Summer Time or Daylight Saving Time

Aviation Acronyms

ABN - Abnormal

ACARS - ARINC Communications and Reporting System

ACM - Air Cycle Machine

ACP - Audio Control Panel

ACT - Additional Center Tank

ADIRS - Air Data Inertial Reference System

ADIRU - Air Data Inertial Reference Unit ADM - Air Data Module

ADR - Air Data Reference

ADV - Advisory

AEVC - Avionics Equipment Ventilation Controller

AFS - Auto Flight System

AIDS - Aircraft Integrated Data System

AIU - Audio Interface Unit

AMU - Audio Management Unit

ANP - Actual Navigation Performance

APPU - Asymmetry Position Pick Off Unit

APU - Auxiliary Power Unit

ARPT - Airport

ASAP - As Soon As Possible

ASI - Air Speed Indicator

A/SKID - Anti-Skid

ATE - Automated Test Equipment

A/THR - Auto Thrust

ATS - Auto Thrust System

ATSU - Air Traffic Service Unit

AWY - Airway

B - Blue

BARO - Barometric

BCL - Battery Charge Limiter

BCDS - Bite Centralized Data System

BFO - Beat Frequency Oscillator

BIU - Bite Interface Unit

BMC - Bleed Monitoring Computer

BNR - Binary

BRK - Brake

BSCU - Brake Steering Control Unit

BTC - Bus Tie Contactor

CBMS - Circuit Breaker Monitoring System

CFDIU - Centralized Fault Data Interface Unit

CFDS - Centralized Fault Display System

CHC - Cargo Heat Controller

CHG - Change

CIDS - Cabin Intercommunication Data System

C/L - Checklist

CO RTE - Company Route

CONF - Configuration (Flaps/ Slats)

CPC - Cabin Pressure Controller

CPCU - Cabin Pressure Controller Unit

CRC - Continuous Repetitive Chime

CRG - Cargo

CSCU - Cargo Smoke Control Unit

CSM/G - Constant Speed Motor/ Generator

CSTR - Constraint

CTL PNL - Control Panel

CVR - Cockpit Voice Recorder

DA - Drift Angle

DAR - Digital AIDS Recorder

DDRMI - Digital Distance and Radio Magnetic Indicator

DFA - Delayed Flap Approach

DIR TO - Direct To

DITS - Digital Information Transfer System

DMC - Display Management Computer

DSDL - Dedicated Serial Data Link

DU - Display Unit

ECAM - Electronic Centralized Aircraft Monitoring

ECB - Electronic Control Box (APU)

ECM - Engine Conditioning Monitoring

ECON - Economic

ECP - ECAM Control Panel

ECS - Environmental Control System

ECU - Engine Control Unit

EDP - Engine Driven Pump

EEC - Electronic Engine Computer

EFCS - Electronic Flight Control System

EFIS - Electronic Flight Instrument System

EFOB - Estimated Fuel On Board

EIU - Engine Interface Unit

EIS - Electronic Instruments System

ELAC - Elevator Aileron Computer

EMER GEN - Emergency Generator

EO - Engine Out

EPE - Estimated Position Error

EGPWS - Enhanced Ground Proximity Warning System

ESS - Essential

EST - Estimated

ETE - Estimated Time Enroute

ETP - Equal Time Point

EVMU - Engine Vibration Monitoring Unit

E/WD - Engine/Warning Display

EXT PWR - External Power

EXTN – Extension

FAC - Flight Augmentation Computer

FADEC - Full Authority Digital Engine Control

FAP - Forward Attendant Panel

FAV - Fan Air Valve

F/C - Flight Crew

FCDC - Flight Control Data Concentrator

FCU - Flight Control Unit

FD - Flight Director

FDIU - Flight Data Interface Unit

FDU - Fire Detection Unit

FF - Fuel Flow

FGC - Flight Guidance Computer

FIDS - Fault Isolation and Detection System

FLSCU - Fuel Level Sensing Control Unit

FLT CTL - Flight Control

FLX/MCT - Flex/Maximum Continuous Thrust

FMA - Flight Mode Annunciator

FMGC - Flight Management Guidance Envelope Computer

FMGS - Flight Management Guidance Envelope System

F-PLN - Flight Plan

FPA - Flight Path Angle

FPD - Flight Path Director

FPPU - Feedback Position Pick-off Unit

FPV - Flight Path Vector

FQI/FQU - Fuel Quantity Indication/Unit

FQIC - Fuel Quantity Indication Computer

FRT - Front

FRV - Fuel Return Valve

FT/MN - Feet per Minute

FU - Fuel Used

FWC - Flight Warning Computer

FWS - Flight Warning System

G - Green

GCU - Generator Control Unit

GLC - Generator Line Contactor

GNADIRS - Global Navigation Air Data Inertial Reference System

GPCU - Ground Power Control Unit

GRND - Ground

GRP - Geographic Reference Point

GRVTY – Gravity

H - Hour, Hot

HCU - Hydraulic Control Unit

HDG/S - Heading Selected

HDL - Handle

HLD - Hold

HMU - Hydro Mechanical Unit

HPV - High Pressure Valve

IDG - Integrated Drive Generator

IGN - Ignition

IMM - Immediate

INB - Inbound

INBO - Inboard

INCREM - Increment

INIT - Initialization

INR - Inner

INTCP - Intercept

I/O - Input/Output

I/P - Input or Intercept Profile

IP - Intermediate Pressure

IPC - Intermediate Pressure Checkvalve

IPPU - Intermediate Position Pick-off Unit

ISIS - Integrated Standby Instrument System

ISOL – Isolation

LAF - Load Alleviation Function

LAT - Latitude

LAT REV - Lateral Revision

LCN - Load Classification Number

L/G - Landing Gear

LGCIU - Landing Gear Control Interface Unit

LGPIU - Landing Gear Position Indicator Unit

LIS - Localizer Internal Smoothing

LK - Lock

LL - Latitude/Longitude

LLS - Left Line Select Key

LNAV - Lateral Navigation

LONG - Longitude

LRU - Line Replaceable Unit

LSK - Line Select Key

LVL - Level

LVL/CH - Level Change

LW - Landing Weight

M - Magenta, Mach, Meter

MAG DEC - Magnetic Declination

MAG VAR - Magnetic Variation

MAX CLB - Maximum Climb

MAX DES - Maximum Descent

MAX END - Maximum Endurance

MCDU - Multipurpose Control and Display Unit

MCU - Modular Concept Unit

MDA - Minimum Descent Altitude

MECH - Mechanic

MFA - Memorized Fault Annunciator

MLS - Microwave Landing System

MMR - Multi-Mode Receiver

MN - Mach Number

MRIU - Maintenance and Recording Interface Unit

MSA - Minimum Safe Altitude

MSU - Mode Selector Unit

N - Normal, North

NAVAID - Navigation Aid (VOR/DME)

ND - Navigation Display

NW - Nose Wheel

OBRM - On Board Replaceable Module

OFF/R - Off Reset

OFST - Offset

O/P - Output

OPP - Opposite

OPT - Optimum

OUTB - Outboard

OUTR - Outer

OVBD - Overboard

OVSPD – Overspeed

P-ALT - Profile Altitude

PB - Push Button

PBD - Place/Bearing/Distance Waypoint

PBX - Place-Bearing/Place-Bearing Waypoint

PC - Pack Controller

P-CLB - Profile Climb

P-DES - Profile Descent

PDU - Pilot Display Unit

PFD - Primary Flight Display

PHC - Probe Heat Computer

P-MACH - Profile Mach

POB - Pressure Off Brake

PPOS - Present Position

P-SPEED - Profile Speed

PPU - Position Pick-off Unit

PR - Pressure

PRED - Prediction

PROC - Procedure

PROC T - Procedure Turn

PROF - Profile

PROTEC - Protection

PRT - Printer

PT - Point

PTU - Power Transfer Unit

QRH - Quick Reference Handbook

QT – Quart

R - Right, Red

RACC - Rotor Active Clearance Control

RAT - Ram Air Turbine

RCDR - Recorder

RCH - Small unit of measurement

RCL - Recall

RCVR - Receiver

R/I - Radio/Inertial

RLSK - Right Line Select Key

RMP - Radio Management Panel

RNG - Range

RNP - Required Navigational Performance

RPTG - Repeating

RQRD - Required

RSV - Reserves

RTOW - Regulatory TakeOff Weight

S - Slat Retraction Speed, South

SC - Single Chime

S/C - Step Climb

SD - System Display

SEL - Selector

STAT INV - Static Inverter

S/D - Step Descent

SDAC - System Data Acquisition Concentrator

SDCU - Smoke Detection Control Unit

SEC - Spoiler Elevator Computer

SFCC - Slat Flap Control Computer

SLT - Slat

SPD LIM - Speed Limit

SPLR - Spoiler

SRS - Speed Reference System

STEER - Steering

STS - Status

SW - Switch

SWTG - Switching

SYNC – Synchronize

T - Temperature

TGT - Target

THR - Thrust

THS - Trimmable Horizontal Stabilizer

TK - Tank, Track Angle

TKE - Track Angle Error

TMR - Timer

TLA - Thrust Lever Angle

TOGW - Takeoff Gross Weight

TOW - Takeoff Weight

T-P - Turn Point

T-R - Transmitter-Receiver

TROPO - Tropopause

TRU - Transformer Rectifier Unit

TTG - Time To Go

UASS - Unofficial Airbus Study Site

UFD - Unit Fault Data

ULB - Underwater Locator Beacon

UNLK - Unlock

UTC - Universal Coordinated Time

VBV - Variable Bypass Valve

VC Calibrated Airspeed

V/DEV - Vertical Deviation

VEL - Velocity

VFE - Max Flaps Extended Speed

VFEN - VFE Next

VM - Maneuvering Speed

VMIN - Minimum Operating Speed

VNAV - Vertical Navigation

VOR-D - VOR-DME

VSC - Vacuum System Controller

VSV - Variable Stator Vane

W - White, West, Weight

WAI - Wing Anti-Ice

WBC - Weight and Balance Computer

WHC - Window Heat Computer

WTB - Wing Tip Brake

WXR - Weather Radar

XCVR - Transceiver

XFR - Transfer

Y – Yellow

ZC - Zone Controller

ZFCG - Zero Fuel Center of Gravity

Glossary

401K: a savings plan that invests part of a paycheck before any taxes are taken out

9/11: the common name for September 11, 2001, when Islamic-extremist terrorists hijacked four American aircraft for suicide attacks against the United States.

A320: a narrow, commercial passenger airplane made by Airbus that has twin engines and can seat up to 220

A380: the largest airline passenger plan in the world with a wide body, four engines and two decks to fit all of its 853 passengers

Abrasion: the result of a hard surface sliding over another one, producing grooves or other damage to the latter

Accountability: responsibility

Aerial Experiment Association: an aeronautical research group formed in 1907 that produced several different aircraft created by its members

Airbus Industries: an aircraft company that builds in several different countries and has holdings in the United State; claims the first digital fly-by-wire airliner, as well as the world's largest passenger aircraft, the A380

Air Commerce Act: the first aviation laws in 1926 that established government regulations on aircraft, pilots, airports, and flight

Air space: the available area of air an aircraft is allowed to fly within

Air traffic control system: ground based facilities and airport towers where air traffic controllers direct aircraft to land and depart runways, fly through controlled air space, and offer advisories to aircraft flying in uncontrolled airspace

Airline Transport Pilot Certificate: See Airline Transportation Pilot Rating (ATP)

Airline Transportation Pilot Rating (ATP): the highest level of aircraft certification a pilot can reach and must have to fly passengers

Airship: a lighter-than-air aircraft that uses gas bags filled with a lifting gas less dense than the surrounding air

Algorithms: a set of rules to be followed in calculations used especially by computers

Attitude: the slope of the three principal points of an aircraft in relation to the ground

Aviation: the design, development, production, operation, or use of an aircraft

Aviators: men and women who work in aviation; pilots

Before Taxi Check: a list of requirements a pilot must do before moving an aircraft out onto a taxiway

Boeing Company Model 247: the first modern airliner

Boeing 314: a long range flying boat type airplane that could cross the Atlantic Ocean

Boeing 747: a wide-body commercial jumbo jet that holds over 400 passengers

Brittle fractures: the fracture of a metallic object or other material where cracks spread rapidly

Check airman: a person who conducts flight checks on an aircraft or in a flight simulator

Check ride: a practical test that must be passed

Collision avoidance: systems or practices that prevent airplanes from colliding with one another or with other vehicles and personnel

Consolidated Vultee Aircraft Corporation: The Vultee Aircraft Corporation merged with the Consolidated Aircraft Corporation to form the Consolidated Vultee Aircraft Corporation in 1943

Contract Air Mail Act: an early aviation law that authorized government mail contracts to private carriers and determined the airmail rates

contractors: a company that signs a contract to provide materials or labor for another company

control towers: a tall, narrow tower with a 360-degree view that provides a safe and orderly flow of traffic around the airport

Convair: an early American airliner with twin engines and room for about 50 passengers

corrosion: rust, deterioration, decay

Crew Resource Management (CRM): a management system that uses resources and human factors and input to make decisions

DC-2: a 14-seat, twin-engine aircraft produced by Douglas Aircraft Corporation in 1934

DC-3: a fixed-wing propeller-driven aircraft in the 1930s and 1940s for up to 28 passengers

DC-4: a four-engine propeller-driven aircraft not as successful as the DC-3, but used by the military as the C-54 and R5D during World War II.

DC-7: a transport aircraft with the last major piston engines used by Douglas that could fly across the United States used from 1953 to 1958

DC-9: a twin-engine, single-aisle aircraft first manufactured in 1965 that was designed for short flights

DC-10: a three-engine wide-body aircraft known as both a workhorse and a death trap; held turbofan engines and a third engine at the base of the vertical stabilize

Decision speed: the critical aircraft speed down the runway to reject takeoff

Dispatcher: worker responsible for sending or receiving reliable messages

Douglas Aircraft Company: an aircraft manufacturer formed by Donald Wills Douglas, Sr. in 1921 and based in California; became McDonnell Douglas in 1967

Drone: an unmanned, or unpiloted, aircraft controlled from the ground

Erosion: wearing away; corroding

F-14: a twin-engine, two-seat, fighter aircraft built in 1970 for the United States Navy called the Tomcat

Fatigue: a weakening of metal due to pressure and small cracks

Federal Aviation Administration (FAA): the national government authority that regulates all aspects of civil aviation; not including the military

Fibromyalgia: muscle or skeletal pain with fatigue, sleep, memory, or emotional issues

First Officer: the second-in-command on an aircraft

Flight attendants: the men and women of an aircrew who ensure the safety and comfort of passengers from the cabin

Flight deck crew: men or women responsible for the flight of the aircraft from the cockpit, including the captain, first officer, flight engineer, and so on

Flight surgeon: the doctor who cares for pilots and crewmembers traveling in air or space

Fly-by-wire: a computer system for controlling the flight of an aircraft or spacecraft that replaces manual (hand) controls

Flying boats: a fixed-winged airplane with a hull and no landing gear made for water takeoffs and landings

Ford Tri-Motor: a three-engine transportation aircraft produced in 1925 by Henry Ford companies

Gravitational force: gravity; or, the attraction of the earth's mass to bodies near its surface

Grievance: complaint

Ground school: a school for learning flight operations and procedures first safely on the ground rather than in the air

Heads Up Displays (HUDS): a transparent, or clear display that shows data without requiring the user to look away from what they are doing

Hijacked: seized or stolen

Hindenburg: a German passenger airship that caught fire during its attempt to dock at Naval Air Station Lakehurst in Manchester Township, New Jersey, on May 6, 1937

Hub: a center of activity much like a small headquarters

Hull: the watertight bottom or sides of a ship.

Hydraulic: moving a liquid under pressure in a tight, confined space.

Jump seat: an extra seat that folds back or away.

Knute Rockne: a Norwegian-American football player and coach from the University of Notre Dame.

L-1049: see Super Constellation.

Legs: a portion or part of a trip. One trip may have three legs; from point A to point B to point C.

Lockheed 1649A Starliner: the last model of the Lockheed Constellation line built from 1956 to 1958 with four powerful engines that could reach 377 miles per hour.

Lockheed: an aircraft manufacturing company known as The Lockheed Corporation, originally founded in 1912 in California, and renamed Lockheed Martin in 1995.

Logbook: a record of important events for a pilot in the management, operation, and navigation of an airplane.

Martin Company: The Martin Company was formed by Glenn L. Martin and made American aircraft for the defense beginning in World War II. In 1995, it merged with Lockheed to form the Lockheed Martin Corporation.

McDonnell Aircraft Corporation: The McDonnell Aircraft Corporation was formed July 6th, 1939 in St. Louis, Missouri by James Smith McDonnell. The company made the military's F-4 Phantom II and the Mercury and Gemini capsule. In 1967, McDonnell merged with the Douglas Aircraft Company to form McDonnell Douglas.

Medal of Honor: America's highest military decoration awarded to U.S. military service Members for acts of bravery during war.

Meteorological: the facts and processes of the atmosphere that influence weather.

Microburst: a sudden powerful air current that usually moves in a downdraft.

Municipal: city or town.

National Advisory Committee for Aeronautics: a United States federal government agency organized in 1915 to promote aeronautical research.

National Transportation Safety Board (NTSB): a United States federal government agency that investigates transportation accidents involving aircraft, ships, and railroads, as well as sometimes military or hazard waste incidents.

NORAD: an acronym for The North American Aerospace Defense Command, which conducts warnings for aerospace (air) and maritime (sea) organizations in defense of North America.

Obstructive Sleep Apnea (OSA): a sleep disorder where breathing stops and starts during sleep, interrupting the sleep cycle and affecting health.

Octane gas: the measure of a fuel's ability to resist knocking or pinging during combustion.

Oil cups: a cup with a wick or valve used for regulating the delivery of oil.

Pan Am: the largest non-government owned international air carrier in the United States from 1927 until 1991, known for innovations like the use of jumbo jets and early computerized reservation systems.

Pension: a company retirement plan from an investment fund where person and usually the employer has contributed into during a career.

Phonetic Alphabet: the code words assigned to each letter of the English alphabet used by the United States military and other organizations: Alfa, Bravo, Charlie, Delta, Echo, Foxtrot, Golf, Hotel, India, Juliett, Kilo,

Lima, Mike, November, Oscar, Papa, Quebec, Romeo, Sierra, Tango, Uniform, Victor, Whiskey, X-ray, Yankee, Zulu

Piston engine: an engine powered by pistons which are moving cylinders and rings that pump up and down inside the engine itself

Probation: a stretch of time known as a trial period

Pushback clearance: permission given from air traffic control to pilots to start and push back an aircraft away from a gate

Regional: an indefinite area that describes a localization; usually an area with in a state or country

Rear pressure bulkhead: the rear component of the pressure seal in the tail section of all aircraft

Reserve: standby, replacements, backup, or spare

Retracted: withdrawn, returned

Seniority: the highest ranking. Seniority is a list of employees in order of hire date

"Seven Seas": the DC-7C made by Douglas for European carriers in 1956 that extended the range of the DC-7.

Shareholders: owners of pieces of a company

Simulator: a machine designed to provide the realistic experience of operating a machine or other system

SmartTaxi: a new cockpit program that places an aircraft icon of the exact location of an aircraft onto an airport diagram using GPS coordinates of the aircraft

Sterile Cockpit Rule: a rule that requires pilots to avoid unnecessary activities like chatting during critical phases of flight below 10,000 feet

Stratoliner: the first commercial aircraft with a pressurized cabin

Super Constellation: the Lockheed L-1049 that was Lockheed's answer to the DC-6 in 1950; was also produced for the United States Navy and Air Force

Thrust: the force which moves an aircraft through the air

Traffic Collision Avoidance System (TCAS): a computer system used to reduce the incidence of collisions between aircraft

Transcontinental: extending across or through a continent

Transponder: a device on an aircraft for receiving and transmitting radio signals

Turbine: an engine with fans or blades that spin from water, steam, or air pressure

Turbofan: a gas turbine engine and fan that uses the mechanical energy from the gas turbine to move air rearwards

Type rating: a special certification requirement for an airplane pilot to fly a certain aircraft type that requires training beyond the regular license

Unidentified Flying Object (UFO): an object in the sky that cannot be identified

Vertical fins: usually the tail section of an aircraft that points upward and stabilizes the aircraft in the air

Zeppelin: a rigid, cigar-shaped, lighter than air, airship that used propellers and sliding weights

Bibliography

"AAL Company Financials." www.nasdaq.com. Web. July 2017.

"Air Traffic By The Numbers." www.faa.gov. Web. July 2017.

"Amelia Earhart." www.biography.com. Web. June 2017.

Atherton, Kelsey D. "Here come the laser helicopters." www.popsci.com. Web. July 2017.

"Average Commercial Airline Pilots Salary." www.chron.com. Web. July 2017.

"Corporate Stats and Facts." www.news.delta.com. Web. July 2017.

Deglmann, Jen. "Top 10 U.S. Operators by Fleet Size." www.mro-network.com. Web. July 2017.

Franklin, Cory. "Commentary: American Airlines Flight 191 still haunts." www.chicagotribune.com. Web. July 2017.

Goyer, Mireille. "Five decades of female pilots statistics in the United States. How did we do?" www.womenofaviationweek.org. Web. June 2017.

Hanna, Jonathon. "Advances In Cockpit Technology That Could Save Your Life." www.flyaomedia.com. Web. June 2017.

Hethcock, Bill. "Where will Southwest Airlines fly next: Hawaii, South America or elsewhere?" www.bizjournals.com. Web. July 2017.

"History Of Southwest Airlines." www.avstop.com. Web. July 2017.

Houston, Sarina. "A Pilot Certificate Can Help You Land One of These Non-Flying Careers." www.thebalance.com. Web. June 2017.

"Number of American Airlines Group employees from FY 2012 to FY 2016." www.statista.com. Web. July 2017.

O'Hare, Maureen, and Neild, Barry. "What are the world's safest airlines for 2017?" www.cnn.com. Web. July 2017.

Paur, Jason. "Sept. 17, 1908: First Airplane Passenger Death." www.wired.com. Web. July 2017.

Ponsford, Matthew, and Glass, Nick. "The night I invented 3D printing." www.cnn.com. Web. July 2017.

Selyukh, Alina. "FAA Expects 600,000 Commercial Drones In The Air Within A Year." 29 August 2016. www.npr.org. Web. July 2016.

"Southwest Corporate Fact Sheet." www.swamedia.com. Web. July 2017.

"The fleet and hubs of American Airlines, by the numbers." www.usatoday.com. Web. July 2017.

"The World's Biggest Public Companies." www.forbes.com. Web. July 2017.

"The World Trade Center." www.skyscraper.org. Web. June 2017.

"Tragedy at Fort Myer." www.wright-brothers.org. Web. July 2017.

"Turbofan Engine." www.grc.nasa.gov. Web. July 217.

Watson, Jack. *This is Your Captain: The Naked Truth About the Person Flying Your Plane.* Florida: Atlantic Publishing Group Inc., 2015.

Winton, Sophie. "Global study reveals travellers would spend $100 on airline ancillaries to personalise travel experience." www.sabre.com. Web. July 2017.

Wong, Maggie Hiufu. "Five cool technology leaps about to change aviation for good." www.cnn.com. Web. July 2017.

Citations

1. "Anchorage, Alaska." http://www.intellicast.com/. Web. June 2017.

2. Brownlee, John. "What It Was Really Like To Fly During The Golden Age Of Travel?" https://www.fastcodesign.com. 2013. Web. June 2017.

3. "Poverty Guidelines. https://aspe.hhs.gov/poverty. Web. June 2017.

4. "Tracking the 87,000 Flights per Day" http://www.natca.org/. Web. June 2017.

5. "Air Traffic By The Numbers." https://www.faa.gov. Web. June 2017.

6. "Airline Safety." https://aviation-safety.net/. Web. July 2017.

7. S.J Findlay, and N.D Harrison. "Why Aircraft Fail." http://www.sciencedirect.com. 2002. Web. July 2017.

8. "Latest Safety Occurrences." https://aviation-safety.net/. Web. July 2017.

9. "Orbital Objects." http://www.nationalgeographic.com . Web. July 2017.

10. Fenwick, Lindsay, and Huhn, Michael. "Criminal Liability & Aircraft Accident Investigation." *Air Line Pilot*, May 2003. p. 17.

11. "Tracking the 87,000 Flights per Day" http://www.natca.org/. Web. June 2017.

12. Wright, Orville and Wilbur. "The Wright Brothers Aeroplane." *The Century Illustrated Monthly Magazine*, Volume 76. 1908.

13. "Tragedy at Fort Myer." http://www.wright-brothers.org. Web. June 2017.

14. "Tallest Towers." http://www.skyscraper.org. Web. July 2017.

15. Kolmar, Chris. "These Are The 10 Best Cities For Pilots." https://www.zippia.com/. Web. July 2017.

16. "Pilot Salaries in 2017: Which Airline Will Have the Highest Pay?" http://www.airlinepilotcentral.com. Web. August 2017.

17. "Jobs and Careers Related to 10 Popular Hobbies." Photograph gallery. https://www.forbes.com. Web. July 2017.

18. Butler, Gary C., Ph.D., and Nicholas, Joyce S., Ph.D. "Health Among Airline Pilots." *Air Line Pilot,* March 2001, p. 16. https://public.alpa.org. Web. July 2017.

19. Adams, Abigail. "Divorce Rate in U.S. Drops to Nearly 40-Year Low." 4 December 2016. http://time.com. Web. July 2017.

20. "Why is the Divorce Rate so High for Pilots?" http://www.airlinepilotcentral.com. Web. August 2017.

21. Deglmann, Jen. "Top 10 U.S. Operators by Fleet Size". MRO-network. *Aviation Week*. 20 April 2017. Web. July 2017.

22. "American Airlines." http://www.airlinepilotcentral.com. Web. July 2017.

23. "Corporate Stats and Facts." 31 July 2017. http://news.delta.com. Web. July 2017.

24. Kruse, Brian. "Fortune names Delta one of the 100 Best Companies to Work For." 9 March 2017. http://news.delta.com. Web. July 2017.

25. "The World's Biggest Public Companies." May 2017. https://www.forbes.com. Web. July 2017.

26. "Southwest Corporate Fact Sheet." https://www.swamedia.com. Web. July 2017.

27. Wong, Maggie Haifu. "Singapore Airshow: 5 ways aviation will change." 25 February 2016. www.cnn.com. Web. July 2017.

28. Polek, Gregory. "Comac, UAC Formalize Widebody Joint Venture." 22 May 2017. http://www.ainonline.com. Web. July 2017.

29. "AF Chief Scientist: F-35s to Control Drones." 20 February 2017. http://scout.com. Web. August 2017.

30. Winton, Sophie. "Global study reveals travellers would spend $100 on airline ancillaries to personalise travel experience." 26 October 2016. https://www.sabre.com/. Web. July 2017.

31. Wong, Maggie Haifu. "Singapore Airshow: 5 ways aviation will change." 25 February 2016. www.cnn.com. Web. July 2017.

Resources

http://www.airlinepilotcentral.com/

http://www.alpa.org/

https://www.aopa.org

https://clearedtodream.org/

https://www.faa.gov/

http://fapa.aero/pilot_resources_job_market.asp

https://www.ninety-nines.org/pilot-careers-resource-center.htm

https://www.rotor.org/Membership/MilitaryAviators/CareerResources.
  aspx

Author Bio

Danielle Thorne is the author of historical and contemporary adventures, young adult paranormals, and more. From pirates to presidents, she loves to research and travel (by air!) while writing poetry, novels, and non-fiction. Some of her work has appeared in places like Arts and Prose Magazine, Mississippi Crow, The Nantahala Review, and StorySouth. She has co-chaired writing competitions for young authors and is active with several online author groups.

A former editor for Solstice and Desert Breeze Publishing, Mrs. Thorne keeps a blog and enjoys meeting readers and writers from around the world through conferences and social media. Currently, she is working on her next piece of fiction. She is a BYU-Idaho graduate, former youth leader, certified diver, half-hearted runner, and unofficial foodie. She lives south of Atlanta, Georgia, with a Mr. Thorne and cat named Finnigan.

Visit her at www.daniellethorne.com.

Index